Tilia

Outdoor

New
Armchair
Octa 6

New
Chair
Eos 12

Chair
Capri 18

Chair
Capri Pad 22

Chair
Gozo 26

Chair
Gozo Pad 30

Chair
Flora PP & PC 34

Chair
Roma PP & PC 38

Chair
Napoleon-XL PP & PC 42

Chair
Napoleon 44

Chair
Tiffany PP & PC 48

Armchair
Flash-R 54

Armchair
Flash-N 58

Armchair
Royal 64

Armchair
Antares 68

Chair
Antares 70

Chair
Antro 74

Table Alu.Base
Antares 70x70 76

Table Alu.Base
Antares 80x80 78

Table Plastic Leg
Antares 80x80 82

Table Alu.Base
Antares 80x120 86

Table Plastic Leg
Antares 80x120 88

New
Table Plastic Leg
Osaka 90x90 90

Table Plastic Leg
Osaka 90x150 92

Chair
Louise 96

Armchair
Louise XL 100

Chair
Specto 102

Chair
Specto Pad 104

Armchair
Specto XL 108

Armchair
Specto XL Pad 110

Chair
Orient 112

Chair
Orient Pad 114

Chair
Orient PC 116

Chair
Rotus 118

Chair
Rotus Pad 120

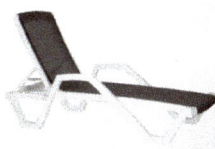

Index

Armchair Octa
New

Immediately giving off a sense of comfort, the soft rounded lines of this single-piece armchair are undoubtedly its most distinctive characteristics. The Octa is an injection-molded armchair made of polypropylene and is reinforced with glass fibers.

It is also lighter because of the woven texture on the back, which is another unique feature of this armchair, further emphasizing the attention to detail. Octa armchair is useful fr both indoor & outdoor and comes up 12 different colours.

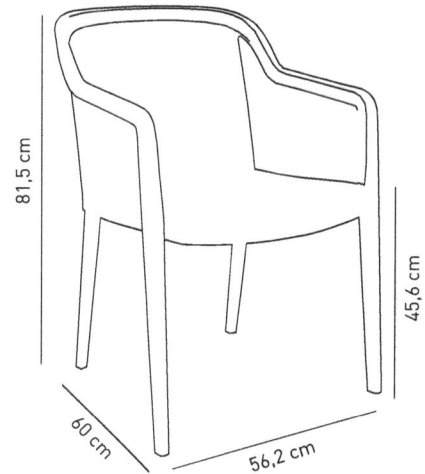

81,5 cm
45,6 cm
60 cm
56,2 cm

Colour Options

Ivory White 101010535
Cream 101010536
Coffee 1010105378
Nile Green 101010538
Tile Red 101010539
Red 101010540
Wood 101010541
Olive Green 101010542
Light Blue 101010543
Turquoise 101010544

Wenge 101010545
Black 101010546

	Crtn	Stack
	Net: 4,62 kg	Net: 4,62 kg
	Gross: 5,30 kg	Gross: 5,00 kg
	20' DC: 260 pcs	20' DC: 480 pcs
	40' DC: 520 pcs	40' DC: 960 pcs
	40' HC: 600 pcs	40' HC: 1040 pcs
	90 cbm truck: 736 pcs	90 cbm truck: 1222 pcs
	4 pcs / crtn	24-26 pcs / stack

Chair Eos

New

The Eos chair is characterized by the smart combination of two different colours with one piece shell in polyproplene. Energetic, elegant and extremely beautiful Eos is the new inspired in the pop art cultures, suitable to be used in almost every kind of environment. Eos is available in 7 different colours polypropylene finishes absolutely combinable. Legs can be knocked down very easily.

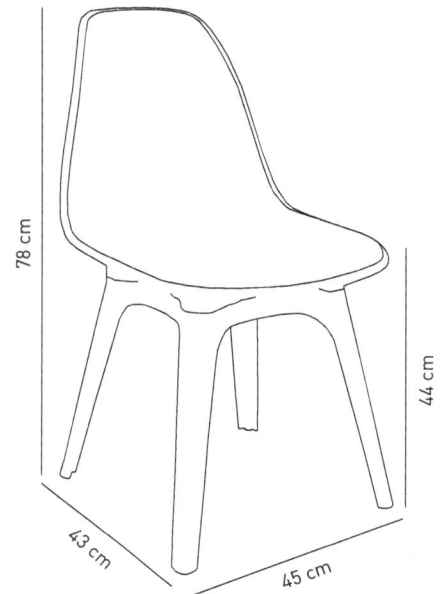

78 cm

44 cm

43 cm

45 cm

Colour Options

Shell   Leg

[] - [] Red/Ivory White-Ivory White 101010548

[] - [] Black/Ivory White-Ivory White 101010549

[] - [] Coffee/Ivory White-Ivory White 101010550

[] - [] Ivory White/Ivory White-Ivory White 101010547

[] - [] Olive Green/Ivory White-Ivory White 101010551

[] - [] Turquoise/Ivory White-Ivory White 101010552

[] - [] Orange/Ivory White-Ivory White 101010560

[] - [] Black/Black-Black 101010553

Crtn

Net: 5,00 kg
Gross: 5,70 kg

20' DC: 412 pcs
40' DC: 824 pcs
40' HC: 960 pcs
90 cbm truck: 1100 pcs

4 pcs / crtn

Red/Ivory White-I. White   101010548

Black/Ivory White-I. White   101010549

Coffee/Ivory White-I. White   101010550

Ivory White/Ivory White-I. White   101010547

Olive Green/Ivory White-I. White   101010551

Turquoise/Ivory White-I. White   101010552

Orange/Ivory White-I. White   101010560

Black/Black - Black   101010553

Chair **Capri**

Our hottest new model Capri chair is stackable up to 14 and is made of 100 % virgin polypropylene applied with gas injection molding. Capri is a monoblock chair with a surface that is slightly wooden textured, light but sturdy at the same time. The characteristic X back is suitable for indoor & outdoor use, in kitchens, restaurants, hotels, gardens, terraces and pool sides. The high-resistant feet have interchangeable PVC footers. It is available in various colors, and you can choose the combination that you prefer.

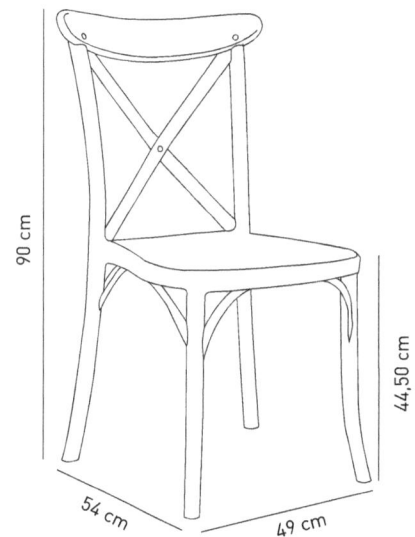

Colour Options

Ivory White 101020376		Wenge 101020377		
Cream 101010228		Black 101020375		
Coffee 101020381				
Nile Green 101020380				
Tile Red 101020231				
Red 101010229				
Wood 101020378				
Olive Green 101020384				
Light Blue 101020385				
Turquoise 101020386				

	Crtn	Stack
	Net: 3,90 kg	Net: 3,90 kg
	Gross: 4,70 kg	Gross: 4,35 kg
	20' DC: 244 pcs	20' DC: 420 pcs
	40' DC: 508 pcs	40' DC: 840 pcs
	40' HC: 612 pcs	40' HC: 1022 pcs
	90 cbm truck: 724 pcs	90 cbm truck: 1250 pcs
	4 pcs / crtn	12-14 pcs / stack

90 cm

44,50 cm

54 cm

49 cm

Scan me

Chair Capri Pad

Our hottest new model Capri Pad chair is stackable up to 14 and is made of 100 % virgin polypropylene applied with gas injection molding. Capri is a monoblock chair with a surface that is slightly wooden textured, light but sturdy at the same time. The Pad provides even more comfort to the chair. The characteristic X back is suitable for indoor & outdoor use, in kitchens, restaurants, hotels, gardens, terraces. The high-resistant feet have interchangeable PVC footers. It is available in various colors, and you can choose the combination that you prefer.

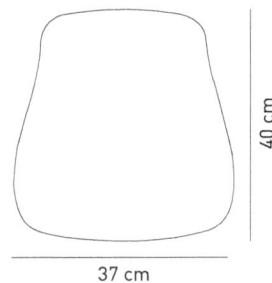

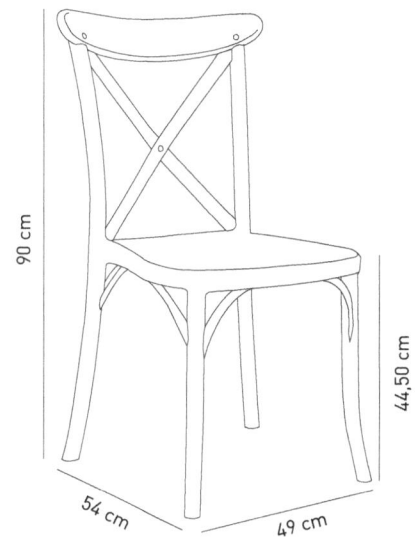

90 cm

40 cm

44,50 cm

54 cm

37 cm

49 cm

Colour Options

Ivory White 101010236
Cream 101010235
Coffee 101010240
Nile Green 101010241
Tile Red 101010242
Red 101010245
Wood 101010243
Olive Green 101010244
Light Blue 101010247
Turquoise 101010248

Wenge 101010246
Black 101010239

Crtn

Net: 4,80 kg
Gross: 5,60 kg

20' DC: 244 pcs
40' DC: 508 pcs
40' HC: 612 pcs
90 cbm truck: 724 pcs

4 pcs / crtn

Scan me

Chair Gozo

A combination of lines which line harmoniously to create a minimal silhouette. The efficient virgin polypropylene with gas assisted moulding technique guarantees solidity and allows to achieve different sections for its back and legs. Surface is slightly wooden textured, light but sturdy and the characteristic back is suitable for indoor & outdoor use, in kitchens, restaurants, hotels, gardens, terraces and pool sides. The high-resistant feet have interchangeable PVC footers. Chair Gozo is an elegant model which can easily fit into different environments.

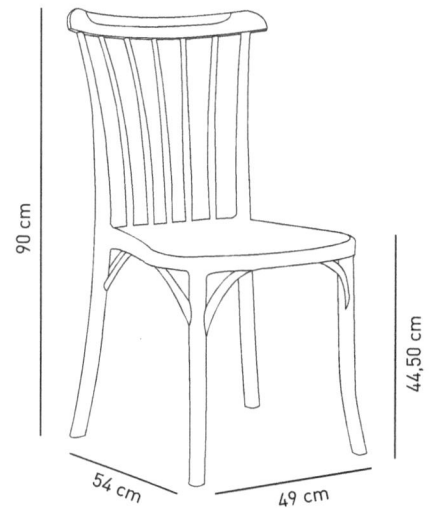

90 cm · 44,50 cm · 54 cm · 49 cm

Colour Options

Ivory White 101020647
Cream 101020399
Coffee 101020393
Nile Green 101020389
Tile Red 101020391
Red 101020392
Wood 101020395
Olive Green 101020394
Light Blue 101020396
Turquoise 101020397

Wenge 101020388
Black 101020387

	Crtn	Stack
Net	3,80 kg	3,80 kg
Gross	4,60 kg	4,30 kg
20' DC	244 pcs	420 pcs
40' DC	508 pcs	840 pcs
40' HC	612 pcs	1022 pcs
90 cbm truck	724 pcs	1250 pcs
	4 pcs / crtn	12-14 pcs / stack

Scan me

Chair Gozo Pad

A combination of lines which line harmoniously to create a minimal silhouette. The efficient virgin polypropylene with gas assisted moulding technique guarantees solidity and allows to achieve different sections for its back and legs. Surface is slightly wooden textured, light but sturdy and the characteristic back is suitable for indoor & outdoor use, in kitchens, restaurants, hotels, gardens, terraces and pool sides. The high-resistant feet have interchangeable PVC footers. Chair Gozo is an elegant model which can easily fit into different environments.

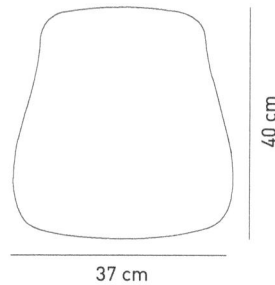

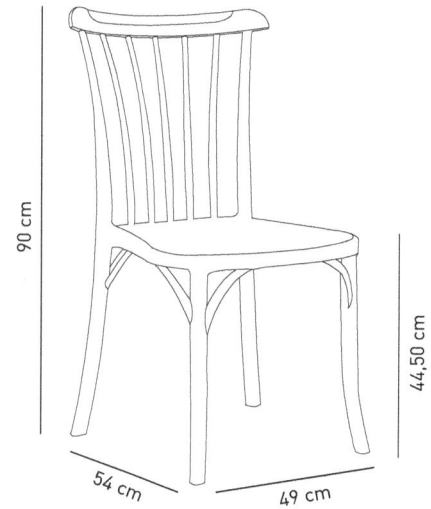

40 cm

37 cm

90 cm

44,50 cm

54 cm

49 cm

Colour Options

☐ Ivory White 101010261
☐ Cream 101010260
☐ Coffee 101010251
☐ Nile Green 101010252
☐ Tile Red 101010253
☐ Red 101010256
☐ Wood 101010254
☐ Olive Green 101010255
☐ Light Blue 101010258
☐ Turquoise 101010259

☐ Wenge 101010257
☐ Black 101010250

Crtn

Net: 4,70 kg
Gross: 5,50 kg

20' DC: 276 pcs
40' DC: 560 pcs
40' HC: 648 pcs
90 cbm truck: 780 pcs

4 pcs / crtn

Scan me

Boyteks Fabric (Indoor Use)

70% Olefin + 30% Polyester

Test ISO 12945-2 (Pilling)

ISO 13936-2 (Seam Slippage)

ISO 12947-2 (Abrasion)

ISO 105x12 (Rubbing)

- Plastic underneath the sponge
- 1 cm / 3 cm 28-HD gray sponge
- Attachable with velcro strip
- Pad thickness : 2 cm / 4 cm
- Pad weight : 0,9 kg
- Pad dimensions : 37x40x4 cm

Fabric Options (Indoor)

Beige 345

Grey 75

Beige 371

Grey 305

Blue 256

Red 302

Black 550

Chair **Flora PP & PC**

Flora PC

Flora PP

Flora chair combines essential design with an exceptionally robust structure to produce the lightness and intangibility of its image. It is produced with gas assisted technology with 100 % virgin polyproplene, polycarbonate stackable up to 11 pcs which let you more space in your wedding halls, organisation areas or hotel ball saloon. Flora is incredibly durable, flexible and suitable for both indoor and outdoor use.

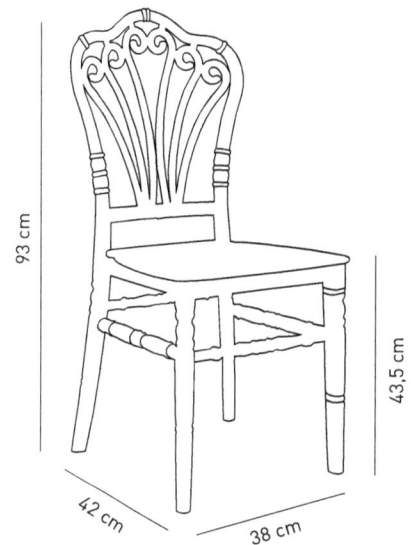

93 cm

43,5 cm

42 cm

38 cm

Colour Options-PP	Colour Options-PC	Stack-PP	Stack-PC
Ivory White 101020700	Transparent 101020705	Net: 3,80 kg Gross: 4,30 kg	Net: 4,80 kg Gross: 5,30 kg
Black 101020702		20' DC: 450 pcs 40' DC: 927 pcs 40' HC: 1133 pcs 90 cbm truck: 1342 pcs	20' DC: 450 pcs 40' DC: 927 pcs 40' HC: 1133 pcs 90 cbm truck: 1342 pcs
Silver 101020704			
Gold 101020703		9-11 pcs / stack	9-11 pcs / stack

PP
Scan me

PC
Scan me

Chair **Roma PP & PC**

Roma PC

Roma PP

A most inviting chair and a baroque style back that inspires comfort, neatness. Roma is the combination of sophisticated design and advanced plastic processing design. Stackable up to 11 pcs which let you more space in your wedding halls, organisation areas or hotel ball saloon. Roma is incredibly durable, flexible and suitable for both indoor and outdoor use.

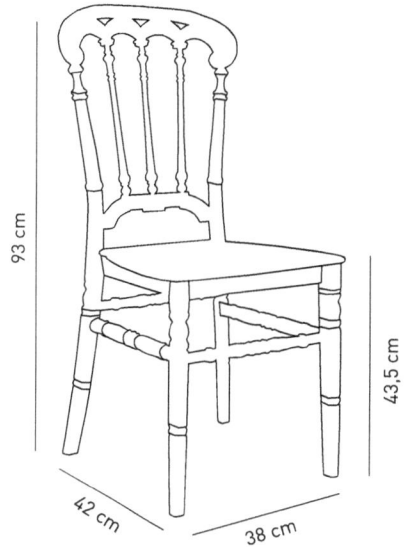

Colour Options-**PP**

☐ Ivory White 101020707
■ Black 101020708
▨ Silver 101020710
▨ Gold 101020709

Colour Options-**PC**

☐ Transparent 101020712

Stack-PP

Net: 3,80 kg
Gross: 4,30 kg

20' DC: 450 pcs
40' DC: 927 pcs
40' HC: 1133 pcs
90 cbm truck: 1342 pcs

9-11 pcs / stack

Stack-PC

Net: 5,15 kg
Gross: 5,65 kg

20' DC: 450 pcs
40' DC: 927 pcs
40' HC: 1133 pcs
90 cbm truck: 1342 pcs

9-11 pcs / stack

PP   PC

Scan me   Scan me

Chair **Napoleon-XL PP & PC**

Napoleon-XL PC

Napoleon-XL PP

This product has CATAS certificate.

Napoleon XL chair is made of monoblock polypropylene and polycarbonate with gas assisted injection technology. You can furnish your space with the contemporary and fabulous Napoleon XL chair. It can be used both outdoors and indoors. Simple to stack up to 11 pieces. It is available in ivory white, gold, silver, black and transparent colours.

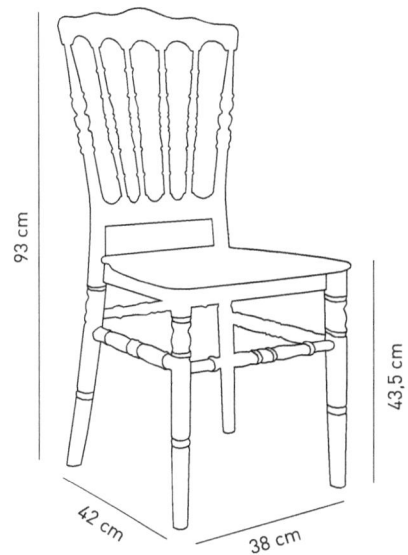

93 cm

43,5 cm

42 cm

38 cm

Colour Options-PP

Ivory White 101020714

Black 101020715

Silver 101020717

Gold 101020716

Colour Options-PC

Transparent 101020719

Stack-PP

Net: 3,80 kg
Gross: 4,30 kg

20' DC: 450 pcs
40' DC: 927 pcs
40' HC: 1133 pcs
90 cbm truck: 1342 pcs

9-11 pcs / stack

Stack-PC

Net: 5,17 kg
Gross: 5,67 kg

20' DC: 450 pcs
40' DC: 927 pcs
40' HC: 1133 pcs
90 cbm truck: 1342 pcs

9-11 pcs / stack

PP
Scan me

PC
Scan me

Chair **Napoleon**

Napoleon chair is made of monoblock polypropylene with gas assisted injection technology. You can furnish your space with the contemporary and fabulous Napoleon chair. It can be used both outdoors and indoors. Simple to stack up to 10 pieces. It is available in white and black colours.

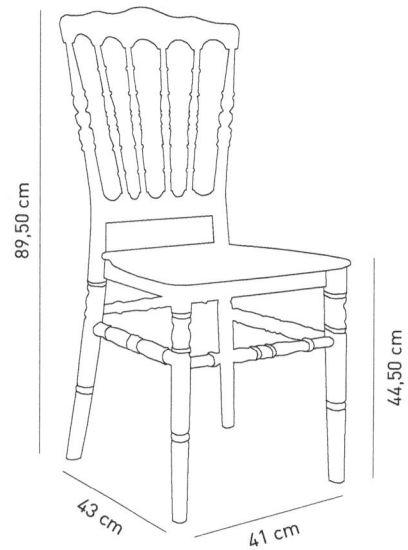

89,50 cm

44,50 cm

43 cm

41 cm

Colour Options

☐ Ivory White 101020644

■ Black 101020359

Stack

Net: 3,80 kg
Gross: 4,30 kg

20' DC: 424 pcs
40' DC: 864 pcs
40' HC: 1080 pcs
90 cbm truck: 1300 pcs

8-10 pcs / stack

Scan me

Chair **Tiffany PP & PC**

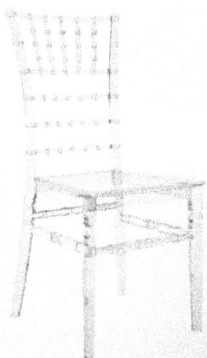

Tiffany PC

Tiffany PP

Tiffany chair is made of monoblock polypropylene, polycarbonate with gas assisted injection technology. Thanks to its elegant look of the extraordinary legs and baroque style it perfectly fits into your dream wedding and organization. It can be stacked up to 11 pieces. It's both perfect for indoor and outdoor usage. It is available in ivory white , gold, silver and black colours. Cushion Uno, Cushion Due, Cushion Tre can be used with the Tiffany chair.

93 cm

43,50 cm

42 cm

38 cm

Colour Options-PP	Colour Options-PC	Stack-PP	Stack-PC
☐ Ivory White 101020643	☐ Transparent 101020720	Net: 3,85 kg Gross: 4,35 kg	Net: 5,20 kg Gross: 5,70 kg
◼ Black 101020345		20' DC: 450 pcs 40' DC: 927 pcs 40' HC: 1133 pcs 90 cbm truck: 1342 pcs	20' DC: 450 pcs 40' DC: 927 pcs 40' HC: 1133 pcs 90 cbm truck: 1342 pcs
◻ Silver 101020343			
▨ Gold 101020344		9-11 pcs / stack	9-11 pcs / stack

PP   PC

Scan me   Scan me

Cushion **UNO**

Side View   Front View   Rear View

- Plastic shell
- Fusing
- 3 cm 28-HD grey sponge
- Mounted to seat with velcro strip
- Fabric Options: Akron, waterproof and artificial leather

Cushion **DUE**

Side View   Front View   Rear View

- 3 cm 28-HD grey sponge
- Zipper
- Mounted to back with velcro strip
- Fabric Options : Akron, waterproof and artificial leather

Cushion **TRE**

Side View   Front View   Rear View

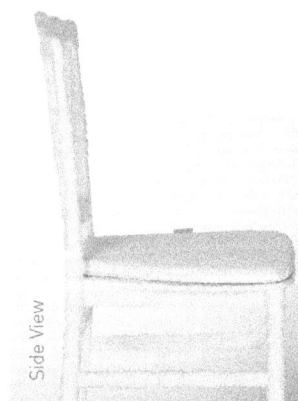

- 3 cm 28-HD grey sponge
- Zipper
- Mounted to back with ropes
- Fabric Options : Akron, waterproof and artificial leather

Boyteks Fabric Options (Indoor)

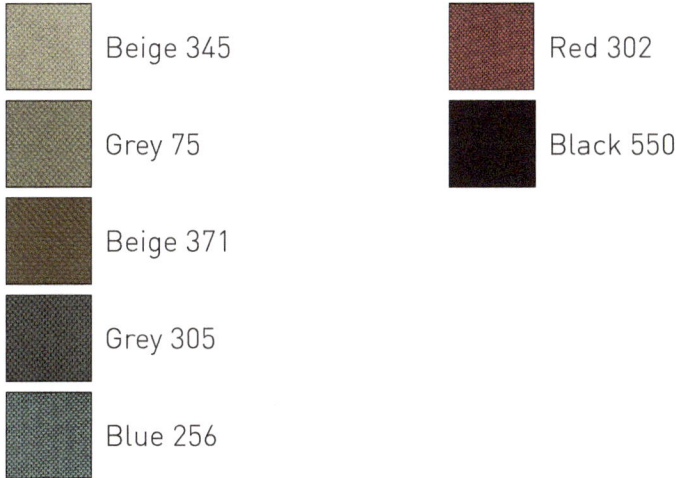

Beige 345

Grey 75

Beige 371

Grey 305

Blue 256

Red 302

Black 550

70 % Olefin + 30% Polyester
Test ISO 12945-2 (Pilling)
        ISO 13936-2 (Seam Slippage)
        ISO 12947-2 (Abrasion)
        ISO 105x12 (Rubbing)

Waterproof Fabric Options (Outdoor)

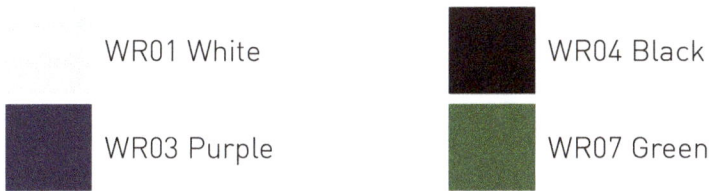

WR01 White

WR03 Purple

WR04 Black

WR07 Green

- % 100 Polyester
- PU waterproof layer
- It should be wiped gently with
  circular motions with a damp cloth

Artificial Leather Fabric Options (Outdoor)

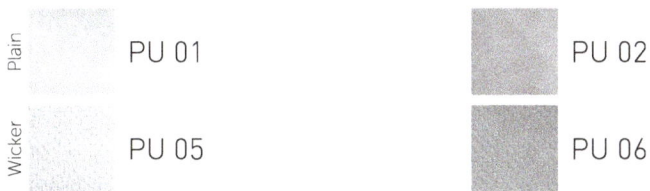

Plain

Wicker

PU 01

PU 05

PU 02

PU 06

- Nature and human friendly
  products can be produced without
  using toxic chemicals which harm
  human health.
- To remove oil stains; use a soapy
  cotton cloth and gently rub the
  stain with circular movements.
- After that use a clean, humid
  cloth to wipe off the area and dry
  the surface.
  To remove dust; use a vacuum
  cleaner or a soft brush.

Tests ISO 2286-1
        ISO 1421-1
        ISO 12947-2-4
        ISO 13937
        ISO 105-B02
        ISO 13936-1-2

Armchair Flash-R

Armchair Flash-R makes your places look more elegant with it's interwoven texture that hides any possible scratches on its surface. It is stackable up to six pieces. The backrest and seat, constructed in wicker, allows this armchair to combine well with various Tilia wicker products like Antares and Osaka tables. Flash is manufactured as a single piece, using gas injection technology. It comes in six different colors; white, cream, wood, wenge,coffee and black.

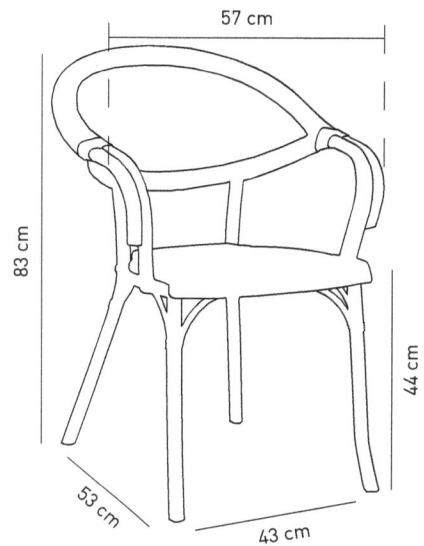

Colour Options

- Ivory White 101010262
- Cream 101010223
- Wood 101010224
- Coffee 101010263
- Wenge 101010225
- Black 101010226

	Crtn	Stack
	Net: 5,20 kg	Net: 5,20 kg
	Gross: 6,10 kg	Gross: 5,70 kg
	20' DC: 188 pcs	20' DC: 336 pcs
	40' DC: 376 pcs	40' DC: 742 pcs
	40' HC: 444 pcs	40' HC: 848 pcs
	90 cbm truck: 568 pcs	90 cbm truck: 1020 pcs
	4 pcs / crtn	14-16 pcs / stack

Scan me

Armchair Flash-N

Armchair Flash -N makes your places look more elegant with it's fabric texture that hides any possible scratches on its surface. It is stackable up to six pieces. The backrest and seat, constructed in fabric, allows this armchair to combine well with various Tilia wicker products like Antares and Osaka tables. Flash is manufactured as a single piece, using gas injection technology. It comes in six different body colors; white, cream, wood, wenge, coffee, black which is combinable with 13 different net colours: beige, beige/coffee, linen, yellow/beige, gold/black, black, smoky, light green, yellow, red, blue, navy blue, dark green.

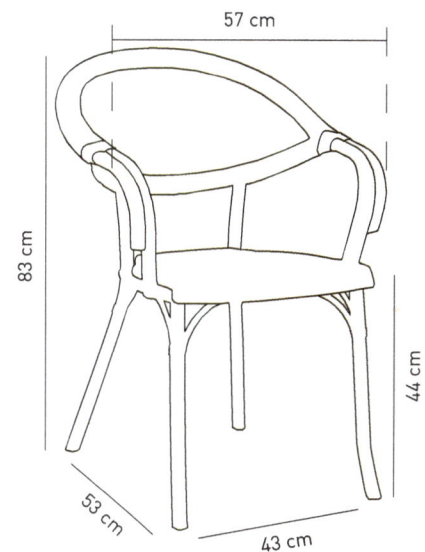

57 cm

83 cm

44 cm

53 cm

43 cm

Colour Options

Ivory White 101010264
Cream 101010265
Wood 101010266
Coffee 101010267
Wenge 101010268
Black 101010269

Net Colours

Beige 0108
Beige & Coffee 0271
Yellow & Beige 0155
Linen 0711
Gold & Black 5247
Black 0400
Smoky 0902
Red 2109
Blue 4219
Navy Blue 4011
Dark Green 3187
Silver & Black 0111

Crtn

Net: 4,50 kg
Gross: 5,40 kg

20' DC: 188 pcs
40' DC: 376 pcs
40' HC: 444 pcs
90 cbm truck: 568 pcs

4 pcs / crtn

Stack

Net: 4,50 kg
Gross: 5,20 kg

20' DC: 336 pcs
40' DC: 742 pcs
40' HC: 848 pcs
90 cbm truck: 1020 pcs

14-16 pcs / stack

Scan me

101020869

Coffee/Red

101020871

Coffee/Yellow

101020811

Ivory White/Light Green

101020876

Coffee/Black

101020821

Cream/Smoky

101020870

Coffee/Beige-Coffee

101020875

Coffee/Gold-Black

101020867

Coffee/Blue

101020805

Ivory White/Yellow

101020801

Ivory White/Blue

101020823

Cream/Light Green

101020814

Cream/Beige

101020816

Cream/Red

101020815

Cream/Navy Blue

101020806

Ivory White/Dark Green

101020831

Wood/Yellow

101020857

Black/Yellow

101020855

Black/Red

101020860

Black/Smoky

101020826

Wood/Beige

101020862

Black/Black

101020839

Wenge/Linen

101020849

Wenge/Gold-Black

101020847

Wenge/Yellow-Beige

101020830

Wood/Beige-Coffee

101020842

Wenge/Navy Blue

101020844

Wenge/Beige-Coffe

101020836

Wood/Black

101020835

Wood/Gold-Black

101020833

Wood/Yellow-Beige

101020845

Wenge/Yellow

101020854

Black/Navy Blue

Armchair Royal

Our model Royal is made of 100 % virgin polypropylene with gas assisted injection technology. Rattan looking chair is produced from a single mould with legs in circular shape. Legs and arms have wooden looking surface. It is very classy and elegant model for your locality. Useful for indoor/ outdoor.

Cushion Details

- Suitable for Royal Armchair
- Sponge thickness : 3 cm / 5 cm
- Zip
- Attaching with rope to leg

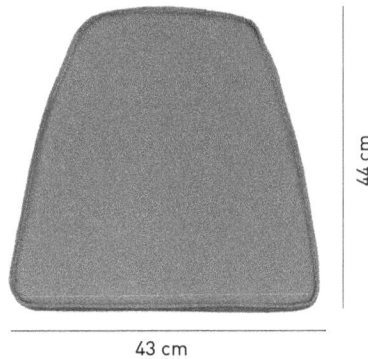

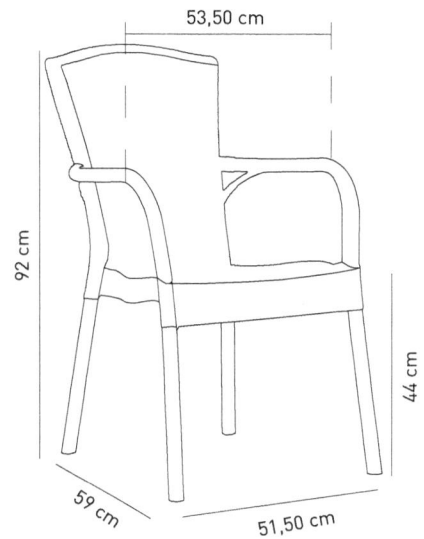

44 cm

43 cm

53,50 cm

92 cm

44 cm

59 cm

51,50 cm

Colour Options	Waterproof Fabric Options (Outdoor)	Crtn	Stack
Ivory White 101010107	White	Net: 5,25 kg	Net: 5,25 kg
Cream 101010102	Beige	Gross: 6,10 kg	Gross: 5,65 kg
Wood 101010103	L.Brown	20' DC: 220 pcs	20' DC: 440 pcs
Coffee 101010106		40' DC: 452 pcs	40' DC: 920 pcs
Wenge 101010104		40' HC: 520 pcs	40' HC: 920 pcs
Black 101010105		90 cbm truck: 644 pcs	90 cbm truck: 1180 pcs
		4 pcs / crtn	20 pcs / stack

Scan me

Armchair Antares

Totally rattan looking armchair is produced from 100 % virgin, glassfibre charged polypropylene and offers you ergonomic and comfortable seating. Six different colours options ; Black, Wenge, Wood, Coffee, Cream and Ivory White. It's a stackable armchair which helps you to gain place. Robustness and strength has already approved by Catas.

Cushion Details

- Suitable for Antares Armchair
- Sponge thickness : 3 cm / 5 cm
- Zip
- Attaching with rope to leg

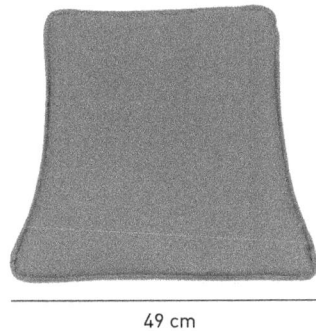

49 cm   44 cm

58 cm   83 cm   45 cm   57 cm   57 cm

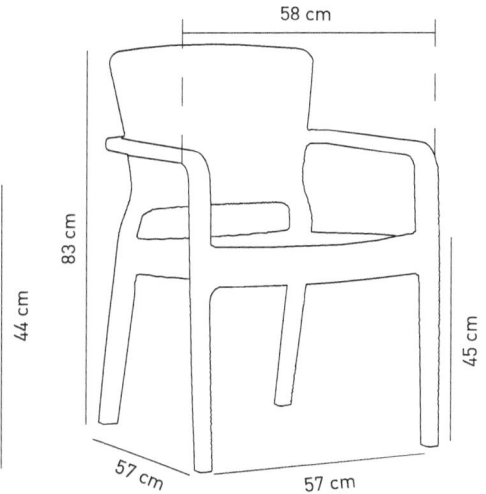

Colour Options

- Ivory White 101010188
- Cream 101010197
- Wood 101010192
- Coffee 101010230
- Wenge 101010156
- Black 101010203

Waterproof Fabric Options (Outdoor)

- White
- Beige
- L.Brown

	Crtn	Stack
Net	4,75 kg	4,75 kg
Gross	5,75 kg	5,05 kg
20' DC	252 pcs	408 pcs
40' DC	536 pcs	901 pcs
40' HC	592 pcs	1007 pcs
90 cbm truck	700 pcs	1160 pcs
	4 pcs / crtn	17-19 pcs / stack

Chair Antares

It is a teammate of Armchair Antares and we believe they complete a high class set together. Chair Antares is characterized by its comfort and 'embracing' seating. The elegance of its design which is suitable for interiors and exteriors. It's a stackable chair which helps you to gain place.

Cushion Details

- Suitable for Antares Chair
- Sponge thickness : 3 cm / 5 cm
- Zip
- Attaching with rope to leg

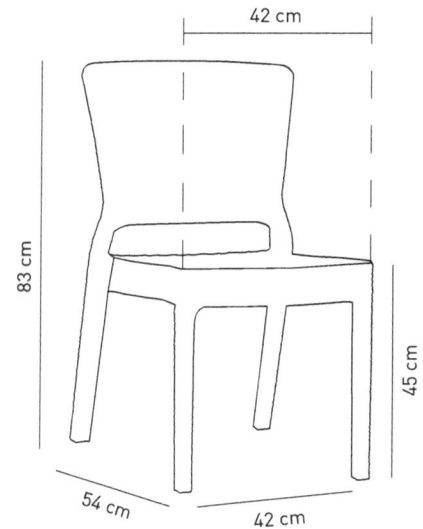

42 cm

44 cm

42 cm

42 cm

83 cm

54 cm

45 cm

Colour Options

☐	Ivory White 101010337
☐	Cream 101010340
☐	Wood 101010342
☐	Coffee 101010338
☐	Wenge 101010339
☐	Black 101010343

Waterproof Fabric Options (Outdoor)

☐	White
☐	Beige
☐	L.Brown

Crtn

Net: 4,00 kg
Gross: 4,75 kg

20' DC: 272 pcs
40' DC: 544 pcs
40' HC: 636 pcs
90 cbm truck: 748 pcs

4 pcs / crtn

Stack

Net: 4,00 kg
Gross: 4,25 kg

20' DC: 408 pcs
40' DC: 901 pcs
40' HC: 1007 pcs
90 cbm truck: 1160 pcs

17-19 pcs / stack

Scan me

Chair Antro

It is designed to combine rattan look with modern shape in a single chair. The result is impressive. It has a completely charming view with its 's-shaped' legs. It is stackable and useful for indoor & outdoor. You can furnish your locality with its six different colors; Black, Wenge, Wood, Coffee, Cream and Ivory White.

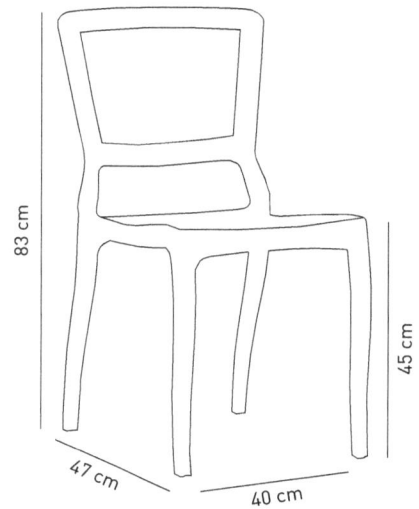

83 cm

45 cm

47 cm

40 cm

Colour Options

Ivory White 101020690

Cream 101020333

Wood 101020335

Coffee 101020651

Wenge 101020332

Black 101020336

	Crtn	Stack
Net	3,20 kg	3,20 kg
Gross	4,00 kg	3,40 kg
20' DC	372 pcs	550 pcs
40' DC	748 pcs	1166 pcs
40' HC	872pcs	1325 pcs
90 cbm truck	1032 pcs	1624 pcs
	4 pcs / crtn	22-25 pcs / stack

Scan me

Table **Antares**
70x70 Iroko top & glass top with central alu. base

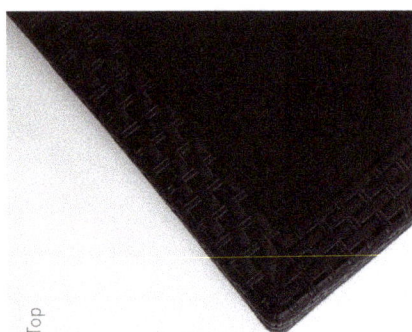

Glass Top

Iroko Top

Table Antares family is an innovation in terms of type and the technology involves in their production. They were designed to create a fantastic combination with Armchair Flash-R, Flash-N, Armchair Royal, Armchair Antares, Chair Antares and Chair Antro. To create more practicality we have mixed plastic with two different materials; iroko & glass. It has an aluminium base for robustness.

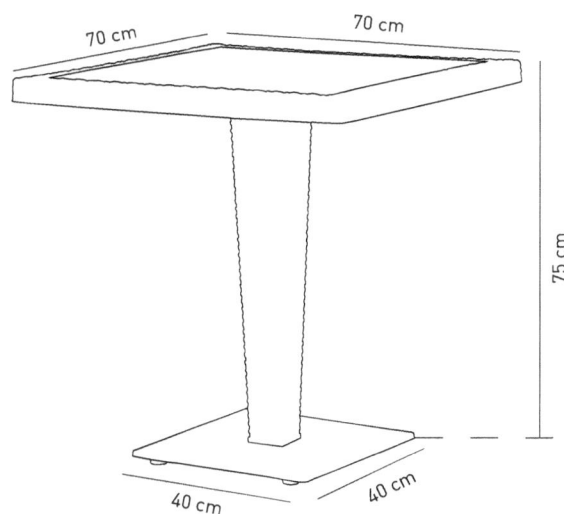

70 cm   70 cm

75 cm

40 cm   40 cm

Iroko Top - Colour Options	Glass Top - Colour Options	Crtn - Glass Top	Crtn - Iroko Top
Ivory White 101020462	Ivory White 101020451	Net: 15,00 kg Gross: 17,00 kg	Net: 14,30 kg Gross: 15,90 kg
Cream 101030104	Cream 101030109		
Wood 101030092	Wood 101030091	20' DC: 370 pcs	20' DC: 370 pcs
Coffee 101030208	Coffee 101030209	40' DC: 740 pcs 40' HC: 850 pcs 90 cbm truck: 950 pcs	40' DC: 740 pcs 40' HC: 850 pcs 90 cbm truck: 950 pcs
Wenge 101030087	Wenge 101030090		
Black 101030122	Black 101030124	3 crtns / set	3 crtns / set

Iroko   Glass

Scan me   Scan me

Table Antares
80x80 Iroko top & glass top with central alu. base

Iroko Top

Glass Top

Table Antares family is an innovation in terms of type and the technology involves in their production. They were designed to create a fantastic combination with Flash-R, Flash-N, Armchair Royal, Armchair Antares, Chair Antares and Chair Antro. To create more practicality we have mixed plastic with two different materials; iroko & glass. It has an aluminium base for robustness.

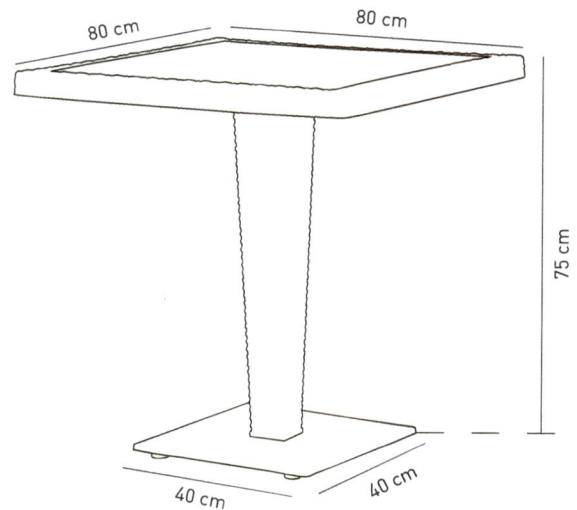

Iroko Top - Colour Options	Glass Top - Colour Options	Crtn - Glass Top	Crtn - Iroko Top
Ivory White 101020450	Ivory White 101020449	Net: 17,30 kg Gross: 18,20 kg	Net: 16,50 kg Gross: 17,40 kg
Cream 101020444	Cream 101020439		
Wood 101020443	Wood 101020438	20' DC: 300 pcs	20' DC: 300 pcs
Coffee 101020436	Coffee 101020435	40' DC: 600 pcs 40' HC: 700 pcs	40' DC: 600 pcs 40' HC: 700 pcs
Wenge 101020442	Wenge 101020437	90 cbm truck: 900 pcs	90 cbm truck: 900 pcs
Black 101020446	Black 101020441	3 crtns / set	3 crtns / set

Iroko   Glass

Scan me   Scan me

Table Antares
80x80 Iroko top & glass top with plastic leg

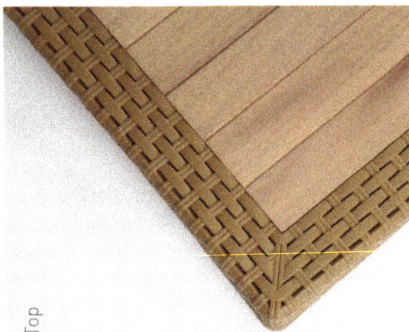

Iroko Top

Glass Top

Table Antares family is an innovation in terms of type and the technology involves in their production. They were designed to create a fantastic combination with Armchair Royal, Armchair Antares, Chair Antares and Chair Antro. To create more practicality we have mixed plastic with two different materials; iroko & glass. It has adjustable pingos for stability.

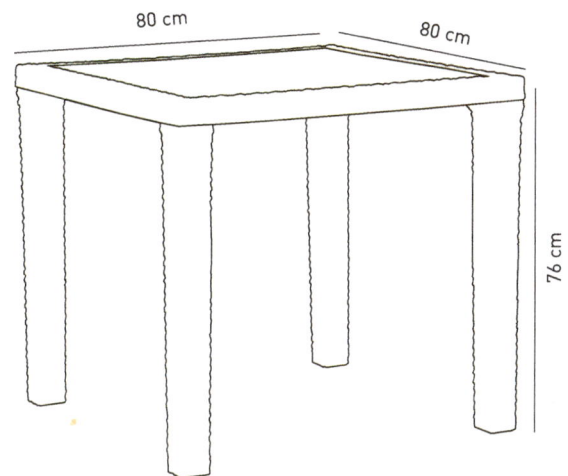

80 cm
80 cm
76 cm

Iroko Top - Colour Options

Ivory White 101020448
Cream 101020429
Wood 101020428
Coffee 101020434
Wenge 101020427
Black 101020431

Glass Top - Colour Options

Ivory White 101020447
Cream 101020424
Wood 101020423
Coffee 101020433
Wenge 101020422
Black 101020426

Crtn - Glass Top

Net: 10,70 kg
Gross: 11,50 kg

20' DC: 370 pcs
40' DC: 740 pcs
40' HC: 850 pcs
90 cbm truck: 1000 pcs

2 crtns / set

Crtn - Iroko Top

Net: 10,00 kg
Gross: 10,70 kg

20' DC: 370 pcs
40' DC: 740 pcs
40' HC: 850 pcs
90 cbm truck: 1000 pcs

2 crtns / set

Iroko   Glass

Scan me   Scan me

Table Antares

80x120 Iroko top & glass top with central alu. base

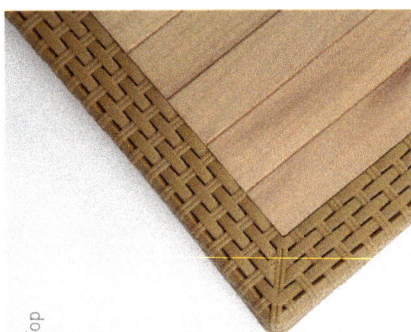

Iroko Top

Glass Top

The big brother of Table Antares family. This model is a necessity for big families and long term friendship chats. It has six different colors; Black, Wenge, Wood, Cream, Coffee and Ivory White. Two different tabletops; iroko & glass. It comes with plastic four-leg base or aluminium central leg just like other family members.

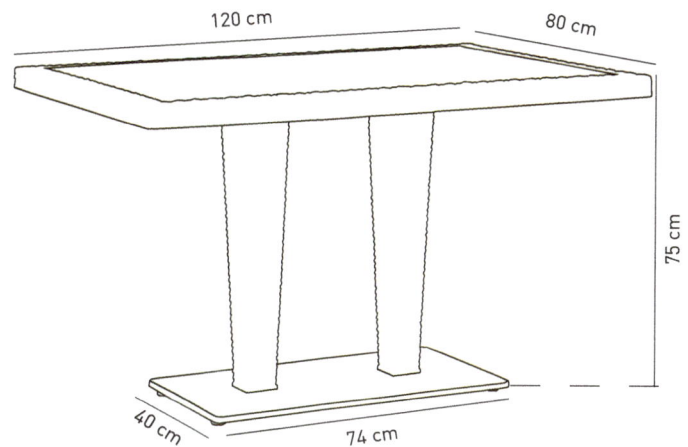

120 cm   80 cm   75 cm   40 cm   74 cm

Iroko Top - Colour Options	Glass Top - Colour Options	Crtn - Glass Top	Crtn - Iroko Top
Ivory White 101020691	Ivory White 101020692	Net: 32,00 kg	Net: 31,00 kg
Cream 101020474	Cream 101020469	Gross: 33,00 kg	Gross: 32,00 kg
Wood 101020473	Wood 101020468	20' DC: 220 pcs	20' DC: 220 pcs
Coffee 101020479	Coffee 101020480	40' DC: 440 pcs	40' DC: 440 pcs
Wenge 101020472	Wenge 101020467	40' HC: 500 pcs	40' HC: 500 pcs
Black 101020476	Black 101020471	90 cbm truck: 630 pcs	90 cbm truck: 630 pcs
		3 crtns / set	3 crtns / set

Iroko   Glass

Scan me   Scan me

Table Antares
80x120 Iroko top & glass top with plastic leg

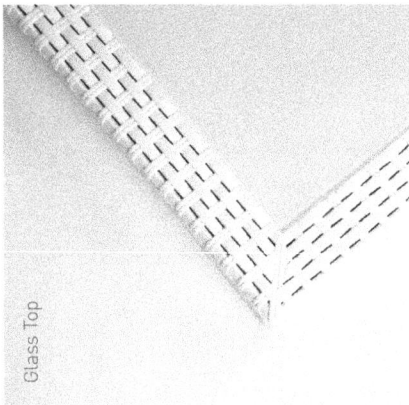

Glass Top

Iroko Top

The big brother of Table Antares family. This model is a necessity for big families and long term friendship chats. It has six different colors; Black, Wenge, Wood, Coffee, Cream and Ivory White. Two different tabletops; iroko & glass. It comes with plastic four-leg base or aluminium central leg just like other family members.

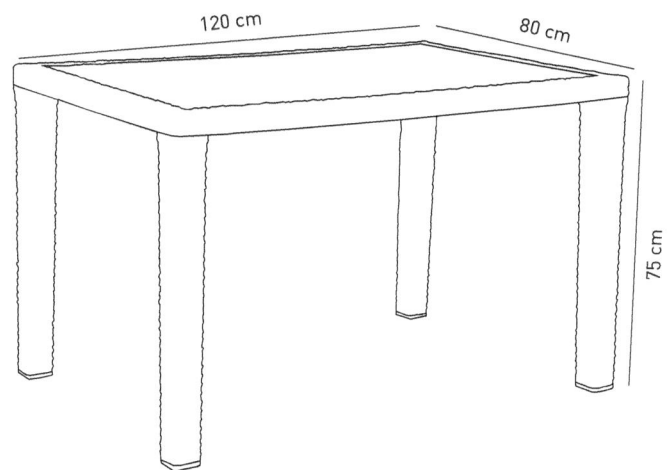

120 cm · 80 cm · 75 cm

Iroko Top - Colour Options

- ☐ Ivory White 101020693
- ☐ Cream 101020459
- ☐ Wood 101020458
- ☐ Coffee 101020481
- ☐ Wenge 101020457
- ☐ Black 101020461

Glass Top - Colour Options

- ☐ Ivory White 101020483
- ☐ Cream 101020454
- ☐ Wood 101020453
- ☐ Coffee 101020482
- ☐ Wenge 101020452
- ☐ Black 101020456

	Crtn - Glass Top	Stack - Iroko Top
weight	Net: 15,00 kg Gross: 15,80 kg	Net: 13,75 kg Gross: 14,55 kg
container	20' DC: 250 pcs 40' DC: 500 pcs 40' HC: 580 pcs 90 cbm truck: 730 pcs	20' DC: 250 pcs 40' DC: 500 pcs 40' HC: 580 pcs 90 cbm truck: 730 pcs
set	2 crtns / set	2 crtns / set

Iroko   Glass

Scan me   Scan me

Table Osaka

90x90   Plastic top & glass top with plastic legs

New

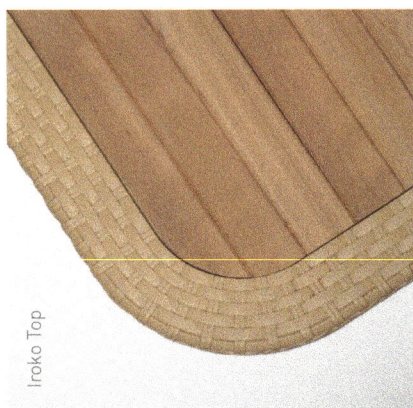

Iroko Top

Iroko Top

This is the new family member of Osaka table range. We tried to combine different materials and different shapes for later join them in a single piece. Different objects working together for a common target; to create a beautiful and stable table.
So this time the top of the table comes in plastic with wooden texture and tempered glass as independent objects which join the top to compose a really harmonious group but always keeping their own identity, always showing their own shape and volume.

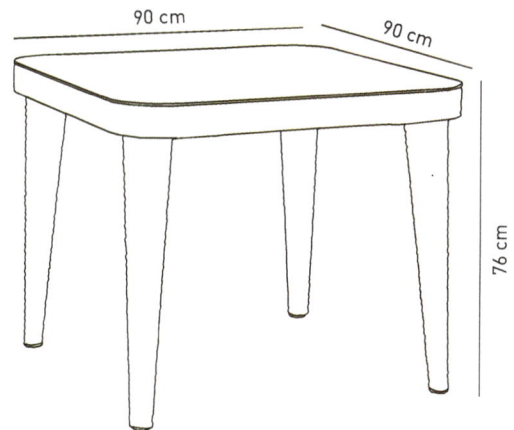

90 cm

90 cm

76 cm

Plastic Top - Colour Options	Glass Top - Colour Options	Crtn - Glass Top	Crtn - Plastic Top
Ivory White 101040151	Ivory White 101040157	Net: 25,00 kg Gross: 28,50 kg	Net: 20,00 kg Gross: 24,00 kg
Cream 101040152	Cream 101040158		
Wood 101040153	Wood 101040159	20' DC: 220 pcs 40' DC: 440 pcs 40' HC: 510 pcs 90 cbm truck: 620 pcs	20' DC: 220 pcs 40' DC: 440 pcs 40' HC: 510 pcs 90 cbm truck: 620 pcs
Coffee 101040154	Coffee 101040160		
Wenge 101040155	Wenge 101040161	2 crtns / set	2 crtns / set
Black 101040156	Black 101040162		

Table Osaka
90x150 Iroko top & glass top with plastic legs

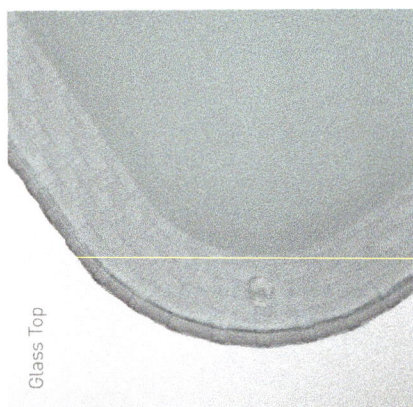

Glass Top

Iroko Top

This product has CATAS certificate.

Giant table. You can use it wherever you want (indoors, outdoors). Table Osaka with iroko/glass top will be the most attractive furniture in your house. Easy to assemble, clean, and carry, it is basically designed to make your life easier. Six different color options are available; Black, Wenge, Wood, Coffee, Cream and Ivory White.

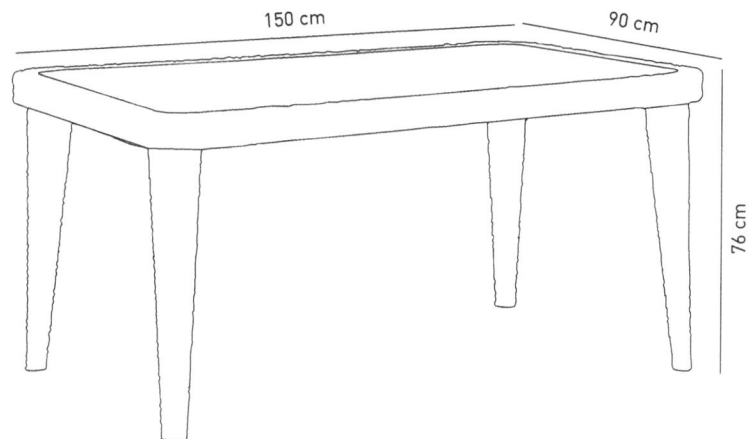

150 cm   90 cm

76 cm

Iroko Top - Colour Options	Glass Top - Colour Options	Crtn - Glass Top	Stack - Iroko Top
Ivory White 101040113	Ivory White 101040119	Net: 30,00 kg Gross: 33,50 kg	Net: 21,50 kg Gross: 24,00 kg
Cream 101040105	Cream 101040101	20' DC: 157 pcs	20' DC: 157 pcs
Wood 101040103	Wood 101040097	40' DC: 314pcs	40' DC: 314 pcs
Coffee 101040107	Coffee 101040112	40' HC: 366 pcs	40' HC: 366 pcs
Wenge 101040106	Wenge 101040100	90 cbm truck: 450 pcs	90 cbm truck: 450 pcs
Black 101040104	Black 101040099	2 crtns / set	2 crtns / set

Iroko   Glass

Scan me   Scan me

Chair **Louise**

Such a noble chair! The elegant and linear design with the fresh colours make Louise a chair that stands out. Chair Louise is made of injection gas moulding polypropylene reinforced by glass fibre. It can be stacked up to 9 pieces.

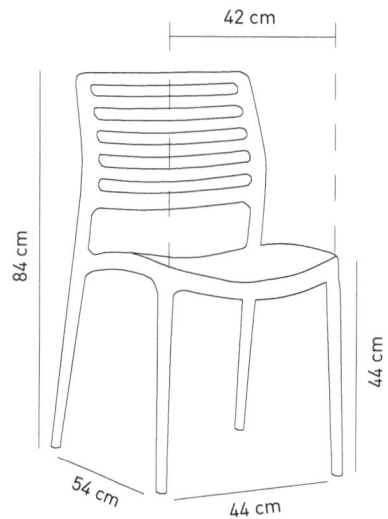

42 cm

84 cm

44 cm

54 cm

44 cm

Colour Options

☐ Ivory White 101020374

☐ Cream 101020289

☐ Orange 101020294

☐ Red 101020295

☐ Pistachio 101020292

☐ Light Green 101020301

☐ Sax Blue 101020291

☐ Charcoal 101020287

☐ Black 101020325

	Crtn	Stack
Net / Gross	Net: 3,40 kg Gross: 4,20 kg	Net: 3,40 kg Gross: 3,70 kg
	20' DC: 300 pcs 40' DC: 600 pcs 40' HC: 708 pcs 90 cbm truck: 852 pcs	20' DC: 525 pcs 40' DC: 1113 pcs 40' HC: 1217 pcs 90 cbm truck: 1418 pcs
	4 pcs / crtn	21 pcs / stack

Scan me

Armchair Louise XL

With customized trim level and ergonomic backrest study, Louise XL is a product designed to ensure durability and functionality. Louise/Louise XL, with and without the armrest, are products that express wide versatility. It has non-slip feets and matt surface finishing. It is produced with gas assisted polypropylene with UV additives.

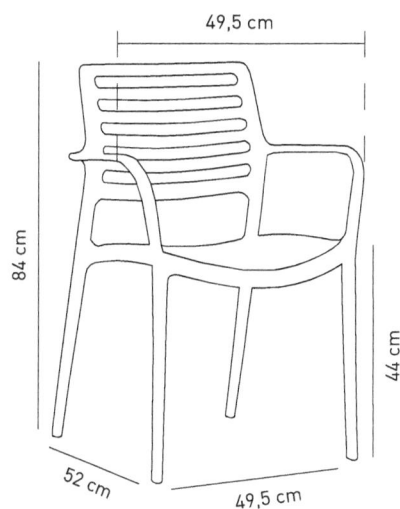

49,5 cm

84 cm

44 cm

52 cm

49,5 cm

Colour Options

☐	Ivory White 101010521
☐	Cream 101010160
☐	Orange 101010165
☐	Red 101010166
☐	Pistachio 101010163
☐	Light Green 101010190
☐	Sax Blue 101010162
☐	Charcoal 101010158
☐	Black 101010202

	Crtn	Stack
Net / Gross	Net: 3,70 kg Gross: 4,70 kg	Net: 3,70 kg Gross: 4,45 kg
	20' DC: 244 pcs 40' DC: 508 pcs 40' HC: 608 pcs 90 cbm truck: 708 pcs	20' DC: 525 pcs 40' DC: 1113 pcs 40' HC: 1272 pcs 90 cbm truck: 1450 pcs
	4 pcs / crtn	21-23 pcs / stack

Scan me

Chair Specto

Chair Specto is made from gas assisted polyproplene and is practical, light and easily stackable. It is available in several colours, which range from warm shades, such as red and orange, to cooler colours such as pistachio green and sax blue, which goes perfectly with every type of furniture for outdoors, dining and relaxation.

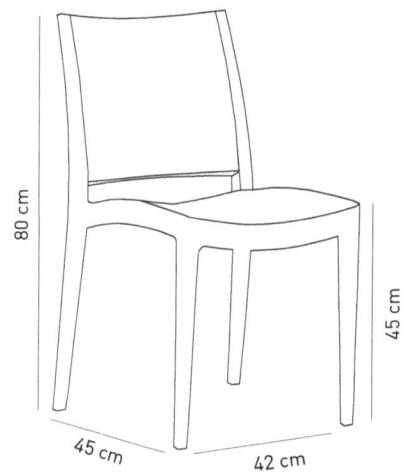

Colour Options

Ivory White 101020884

Cream 101020031

Orange 101020036

Red 101020037

Pistachio 101020034

Light Green 101020203

Sax Blue 101020033

Charcoal 101020029

Black 101020316

Coffee 101040118

	Crtn	Stack
	Net: 2,90 kg	Net: 2,90 kg
	Gross: 3,60 kg	Gross: 3,20 kg
	20' DC: 392 pcs	20' DC: 598 pcs
	40' DC: 816 pcs	40' DC: 1219 pcs
	40' HC: 848 pcs	40' HC: 1431 pcs
	90 cbm truck: 1000 pcs	90 cbm truck: 1680 pcs
	4 pcs / crtn	23-27 pcs / stack

Scan me

Chair Specto Pad

Chair Specto with a slim pad. Its pad is formed by plywood underneath, with a 3 mm thick sponge and water repellent / velvet fabric. The pad is assembled before packaging and the chair is sent to you 4 pieces in a carton box. You can easily use it for both indoors and outdoors.

Cushion Details

- 100 % Polyester
- PU waterproof layer
- It should be wiped gently and circular with a damp cloth

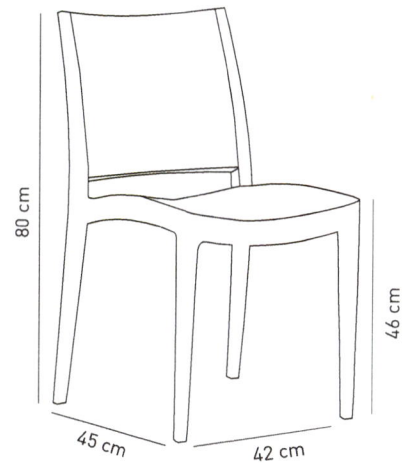

80 cm · 46 cm · 45 cm · 42 cm

Colour Options

Ivory White 101020885
Cream 101040090
Orange 101040092
Red 101040089
Pistachio 101040087
Light Green 101040094
Sax Blue 101040093
Charcoal 101040086
Black 101040095
Coffee 101010510

Waterproof Fabric Options (Outdoor)

Beige 345
Grey 75
Beige 371
Grey 305
Blue 256
Red 302
Black 550

Crtn

Net: 4,00 kg
Gross: 4,70 kg

20' DC: 392 pcs
40' DC: 816 pcs
40' HC: 848 pcs
90 cbm truck: 1000 pcs

4 pcs / crtn

Scan me

Armchair Specto XL

Adaptability to indoor and outdoor environments and stackability make the Armchair Specto XL a classic. It is made from polypropylene reinforced with glass fibers and injection moulded with the use of gas technology. The armchair is solid and light at the same time.

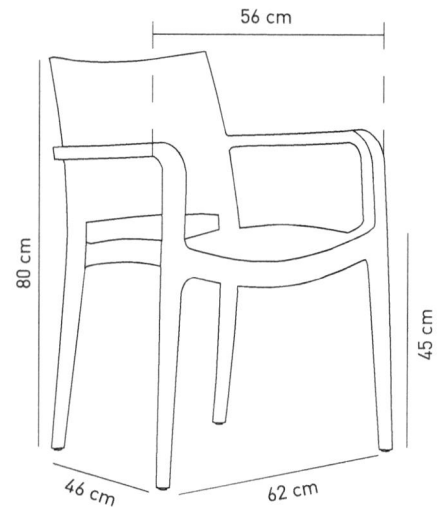

56 cm

80 cm

45 cm

46 cm

62 cm

Colour Options

☐ Ivory White 101010554
☐ Cream 101010173
☐ Orange 101010178
☐ Red 101010179
☐ Pistachio 101010176
☐ Light Green 101010191
☐ Sax Blue 101010175

	Crtn	Stack
	Net: 4,10 kg	Net: 4,10 kg
	Gross: 5,00 kg	Gross: 4,40 kg
	20' DC: 264 pcs	20' DC: 550 pcs
	40' DC: 536 pcs	40' DC: 1166 pcs
	40' HC: 620 pcs	40' HC: 1325 pcs
	90 cbm truck: 748 pcs	90 cbm truck: 1508 pcs
	4 pcs / crtn	22-25 pcs / stack

Scan me

Armchair Specto XL Pad

Specto XL's practicality is combined with the comfort of the Pad. Its pad is formed by plywood underneath, with a 3 mm thick sponge and water repellent fabric. It can be used both indoors and outdoors.

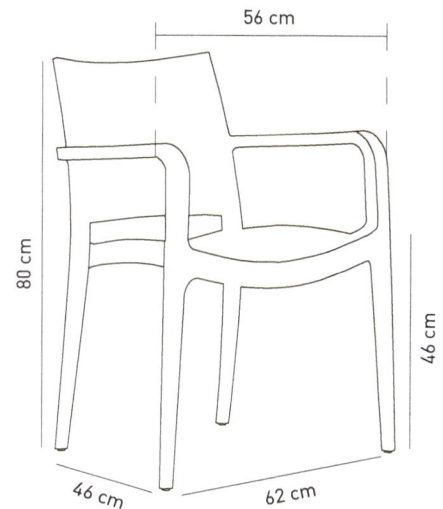

56 cm
80 cm
46 cm
46 cm
62 cm

Cushion Details

- 100 % Polyester
- PU waterproof layer
- It should be wiped gently and circular with a damp cloth

Colour Options	Waterproof Fabric Options (Outdoor)	Crtn
Ivory White 101030215	Beige 345	Net: 4,75 kg Gross: 5,65 kg
Cream 101010156	Grey 75	
Orange 101030161	Beige 371	20' DC: 264 pcs
Red 101030164	Grey 305	40' DC: 536 pcs 40' HC: 620 pcs
Pistachio 101030165	Blue 256	90 cbm truck: 748 pcs
Light Green 101030159	Red 302	
Sax Blue 101030162	Black 550	4 pcs / crtn

Scan me

Chair **Orient**

On its four slim s-shaped legs, Chair Orient is big and comfy. The back of the chair is naturally distinctive and designed to grasp your back completely. Chair Orient is light, practical and it comes in various colours. It can be stacked and used outdoors as well.

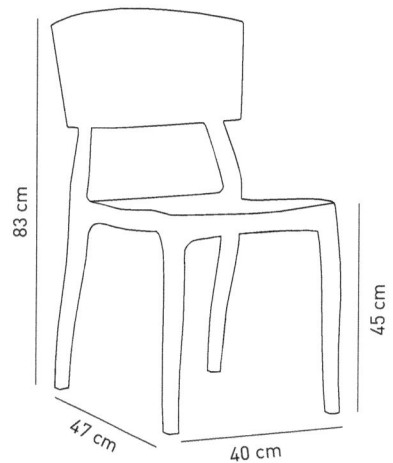

83 cm
45 cm
47 cm
40 cm

Colour Options

☐ Ivory White 101020886
☐ Cream 101020004
☐ Pistachio 101020007
☐ Light Blue 101020011
☐ Yellow 101020008

	Crtn	Stack
Net:	3,65 kg	3,65 kg
Gross:	4,40 kg	4,00 kg
20' DC:	372 pcs	550 pcs
40' DC:	748 pcs	1166 pcs
40' HC:	872 pcs	1378 pcs
90 cbm truck:	1032 pcs	1624 pcs
	4 pcs / crtn	22-26 pcs / stack

Scan me

Chair Orient Pad

Chair Orient Pad is a new member of the Chair Orient family. It is a chair with five different shell colours (Cream, Ivory White, Yellow, Pistachio, and Light Blue) and water repellent fabric. It is perfect for home, office and for contract use.

Cushion Details

- 100 % Polyester
- PU waterproof layer
- It should be wiped gently and circular with a damp cloth

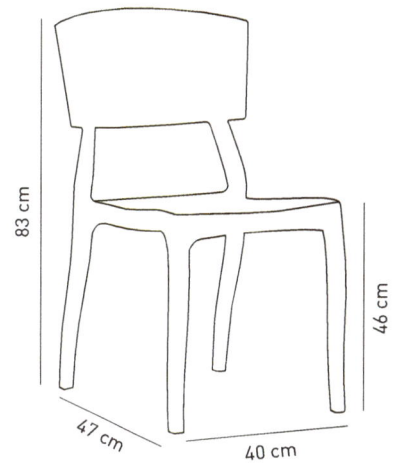

83 cm

46 cm

47 cm

40 cm

Colour Options

- Ivory White 101040149
- Cream 101040059
- Pistachio 101040060
- Light Blue 101040062
- Yellow 101040058

Waterproof Fabric Options (Outdoor)

- Beige 345
- Grey 75
- Beige 371
- Grey 305
- Blue 256
- Red 302
- Black 550

Crtn

Net: 4,80 kg
Gross: 5,50 kg

20' DC: 372 pcs
40' DC: 748 pcs
40' HC: 872 pcs
90 cbm truck: 1032 pcs

4 pcs / crtn

Scan me

Chair Orient PC

Eclectic and versatile, contemporary and elegant in details of its finishes and materials, Chair Orient PC is a brand new product created for collective areas. Its functionality, together with its unquestionable Tilia style, is complemented by the good quality for a unique contract seat that is one of a kind. It's ornamental design gives more folk looking to chair and can be useful for indoor/outdoor.

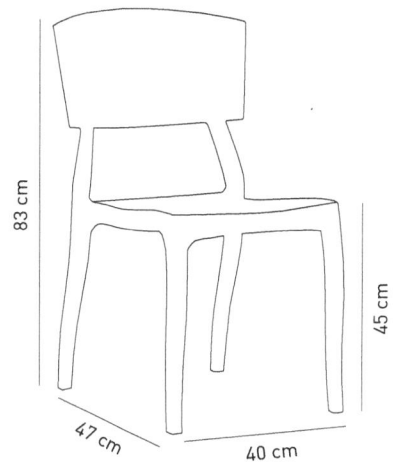

83 cm

45 cm

47 cm

40 cm

Colour Options

☐ Ivory White-Transparent 101020887

▨ Ivory White-Orange 101020888

▨ Ivory White-Red 101020889

▨ Ivory White-Blue 101020890

☐ Cream-Transparent 101020043

▨ Cream-Orange 101020042

▨ Cream-Blue 101020416

▨ Cream-Red 101020044

	Crtn	Stack
Net:	3,25 kg	3,25 kg
Gross:	4,00 kg	3,60 kg
20' DC:	372 pcs	550 pcs
40' DC:	748 pcs	1166 pcs
40' HC:	872 pcs	1378 pcs
90 cbm truck:	1032 pcs	1624 pcs
	4 pcs / crtn	22-26 pcs / stack

Scan me

Chair Rotus

With its minimal and clean design, this chair is reminiscent of an art deco mood. It brings a touch of personality and originality to any ambiance. It comes in five different colours; Cream, Ivory White, Yellow, Pistachio, Light Blue.

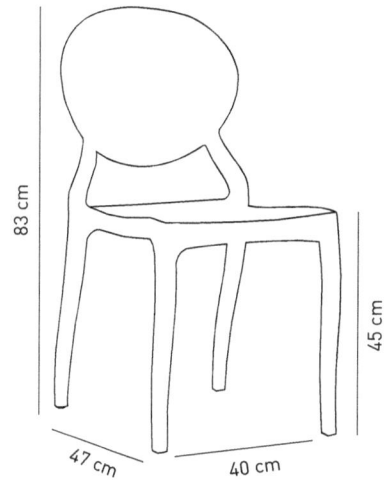

83 cm

45 cm

47 cm

40 cm

Colour Options

☐ Ivory White 101020891

☐ Cream 101020018

☐ Pistachio 101020021

☐ Light Blue 101020025

☐ Yellow 101020022

	Crtn	Stack
Net:	3,75 kg	3,75 kg
Gross:	4,50 kg	4,20 kg
20' DC:	392 pcs	550 pcs
40' DC:	788 pcs	1166 pcs
40' HC:	916 pcs	1378 pcs
90 cbm truck:	1084 pcs	1624 pcs
	4 pcs / crtn	22-26 pcs / stack

Chair Rotus Pad

A chair which combines the elegance of its perfect proportions to the comfort of the seat. The seat is upholstered and contains a polypropylene shell with a sandy surface. The upholstery is water repellent fabric. Rotus is stackable. The upholstery range in combination with the colours of the shell offers a wide range of possible customizations and solutions for both residential and contract furnishings.

Cushion Details

- 100 % Polyester
- PU waterproof layer
- It should be wiped gently and circular with a damp cloth

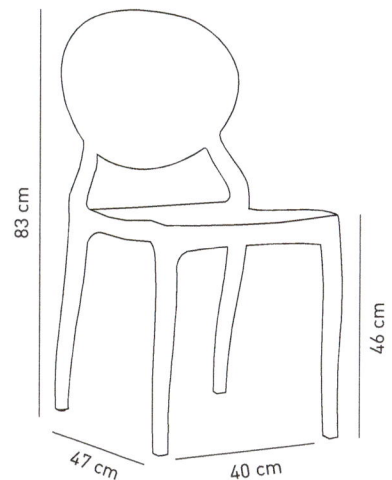

83 cm
46 cm
47 cm
40 cm

Colour Options

Ivory White 101040150
Cream 101040071
Pistachio 101040072
Light Blue 101040074
Yellow 101040070

Waterproof Fabric Options (Outdoor)

Beige 345
Grey 75
Beige 371
Grey 305
Blue 256
Red 302
Black 550

Crtn

Net: 5,40 kg
Gross: 6,10 kg

20' DC: 392 pcs
40' DC: 788 pcs
40' HC: 916 pcs
90 cbm truck: 1084 pcs

4 pcs / crtn

Scan me

Chair Rotus PC

Tilia presents the latest evolution in transparency. A chair offering perfect ergonomic seating combining flexibility and solidity. With transparent PC back, it gives attractive play of light and reflections. Available in many combinations. Orient PC is perfect for the home, office and especially for contract use.

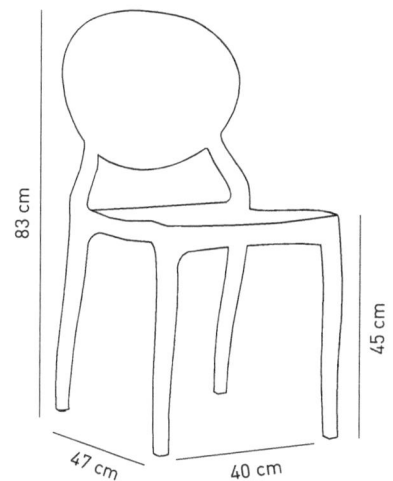

83 cm

45 cm

47 cm

40 cm

Colour Options

Ivory White-Transparent 101020892

Ivory White-Orange 101020893

Ivory White-Red 101020894

Ivory White-Blue 101020895

Cream-Transparent 101020284

Cream-Orange 101020050

Cream-Blue 101020051

Cream-Red 101020052

	Crtn	Stack
Net: Gross:	Net: 3,40 kg Gross: 4,10 kg	Net: 3,40 kg Gross: 3,80 kg
	20' DC: 392 pcs 40' DC: 788 pcs 40' HC: 916 pcs 90 cbm truck: 1084 pcs	20' DC: 550 pcs 40' DC: 1166 pcs 40' HC: 1378 pcs 90 cbm truck: 1624 pcs
	4 pcs / crtn	22-26 pcs / stack

Scan me

Chair Neptun

Refined aesthetics, great comfort, lightness and sturdiness. Light, stackable, available in outdoor version: besides being ideal for domestic use, Chair Neptun is also perfect for public settings. Stacking chair with or without armrests, die-cast aluminium frame. Fiberglass reinforced polypropylene seat and back in cream, yellow, orange, red, sax blue and black colours.

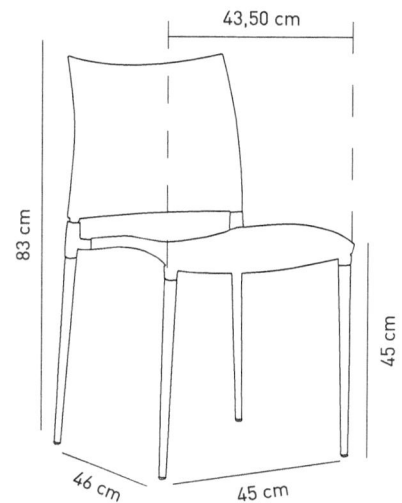

43,50 cm

83 cm

45 cm

46 cm   45 cm

Colour Options

Cream 101020059
Yellow 101020061
Sax Blue 101020060
Orange 101020064
Red 101020065
Black 101020063

Crtn

Net: 4,25 kg
Gross: 5,00 kg

20' DC: 412 pcs
40' DC: 824 pcs
40' HC: 964 pcs
90 cbm truck: 1020 pcs

4 pcs / crtn

Scan me

Chair Neptun PC

Sinuous and sharp corners, clean and functional, chair "Neptun PC", named after its polycarbonate back which characterizes the product. It represents the ideal solution for a light seating and great robustness. Its stackable and also suitable for outdoor use. Glossy finishes available in; orange, sax blue, red, matte finishes available in; cream, red, orange, black and sax blue colours.

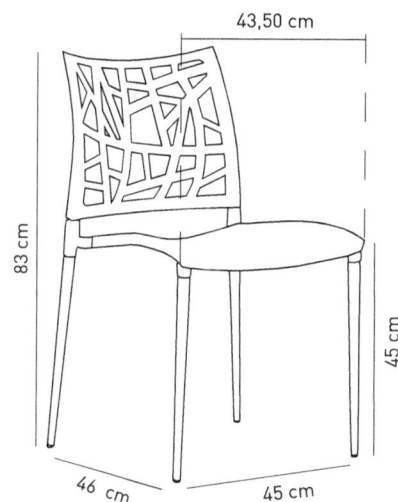

43,50 cm

83 cm

45 cm

46 cm

45 cm

Colour Options

☐ Cream-Cream 101020072
☐ Cream-Orange 101020069
☐ Cream-Sax Blue 101020070
☐ Red-Red 101020073
☐ Sax Blue-Blue 101020076
☐ Black-Black 101020075
☐ Orange-Orange 101020074

Crtn

Net: 4,00 kg
Gross: 4,70 kg

20' DC: 412 pcs
40' DC: 824 pcs
40' HC: 964 pcs
90 cbm truck: 1020 pcs

4 pcs / crtn

Scan me

Armchair Neptun

Refined aesthetics, great comfort, lightness and sturdiness. Light, stackable, suitable for outdoor use: besides being ideal for domestic use, Armchair Neptun is also perfect for public settings. Stacking chair with or without armrests, die-cast aluminium frame. Fiberglass reinforced polypropylene seat and back in cream, yellow, orange, red, sax blue and black colours.

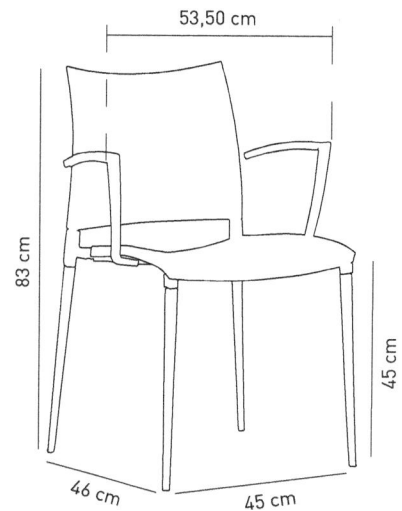

53,50 cm

83 cm

45 cm

46 cm

45 cm

Colour Options

☐ Cream 101010001
☐ Yellow 101010003
☐ Sax Blue 101010002
☐ Orange 101010006
☐ Red 101010007
■ Black 101010005

Crtn

Net: 5,30 kg
Gross: 6,10 kg

20' DC: 336 pcs
40' DC: 668 pcs
40' HC: 752 pcs
90 cbm truck: 888 pcs

4 pcs / crtn

Scan me

Chair Laser

Built on a metal base Chair Laser is a single curvy body made of polypropylene. Spacious and comfortable, the seat fits perfectly in kitchen and dining room. Also ideal in public and community spaces, from clubs to restaurants, to waiting rooms.

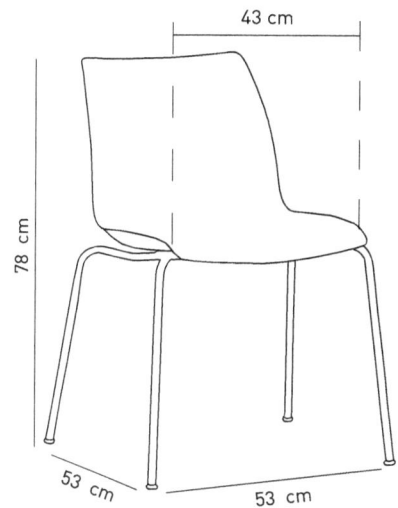

43 cm

78 cm

53 cm

53 cm

Colour Options

- [ ] Ivory White 101020896
- [ ] Cream 101020132
- [ ] Red 101020133
- [ ] Wood 101020204
- [ ] Wenge 101020135
- [ ] Black 101020134

Crtn

Net: 4,30 kg
Gross: 5,20 kg

20' DC: 292 pcs
40' DC: 584 pcs
40' HC: 682 pcs
90 cbm truck: 720 pcs

4 pcs / crtn

Armchair Laser

Armchair Laser conceived from the desire of creating a rational piece of furniture suitable to be placed even in the most characteristic spaces, respecting their style. Matte finished polypropylene shell and Ø14mm chrome tube frame. Cream, Ivory white, red, wenge and black colours available for shell.

58 cm

80 cm

44 cm

47,50 cm

50 cm

Colour Options

☐ Ivory White 101010555
☐ Cream 101010067
☐ Red 101010068
☐ Wood 101010353
☐ Wenge 101010070
☐ Black 101010069

Crtn

Net: 5,50 kg
Gross: 6,40 kg

20' DC: 292 pcs
40' DC: 584 pcs
40' HC: 682 pcs
90 cbm truck: 720 pcs

4 pcs / crtn

Scan me

Bar Chair Laser

Bar Chair Laser, versatile with polypropylene shell available in 6 colours: ivory white, cream, red, wood, wenge and black. Stackable, matte finish shell and chrome frame. It is suitable for indoor / outdoor use.

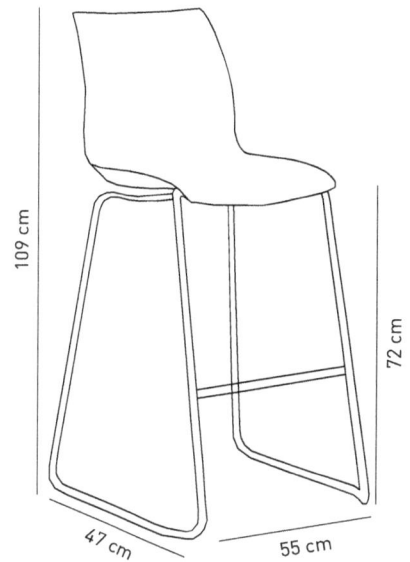

109 cm

72 cm

47 cm

55 cm

Colour Options

- Ivory White 101010556
- Cream 101020327
- Red 101020329
- Wood 101010111
- Wenge 101020330
- Black 101020328

Crtn

Net: 6,00 kg
Gross: 7,15 kg

20' DC: 240 pcs
40' DC: 480 pcs
40' HC: 560 pcs
90 cbm truck: 700 pcs

4 pcs / crtn

Scan me

Chair Max PC

Form & Function in a harmony. Its elegant lines, sober colours and practical usage make Chair Max PC extremely versatile chair, capable of satisfying the widest demands of the business and residential market. Besides its form function its polycarbonate handle makes product easy to carry. Thanks to its intelligent design, Chair Max PC can be stacked up to six.

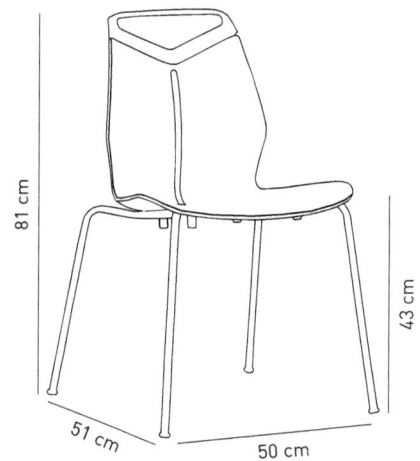

81 cm · 43 cm · 51 cm · 50 cm

Colour Options

Cream-Orange 101020111
Cream-Blue 101020117
Cream-Red 101020109
Ivory White-Red 101020897
Red-Red 101020110
Orange-Orange 101020113
Black-Black 101020217
Sax Blue-Blue 101020114
Wenge-Orange 101020112

Crtn

Net: 4,20 kg
Gross: 5,10 kg

20' DC: 332 pcs
40' DC: 664 pcs
40' HC: 776 pcs
90 cbm truck: 916 pcs

4 pcs / crtn

Scan me

Bar Chair Max PC

The unitized polypropylene seat and polycarbonate handle is attached to chromed structure.It can be useful for houses, workshops, waiting rooms, bars and restaurants.Frequently requested for houses, this product is finally able to satisfy the demands of even the most specific contract customers.

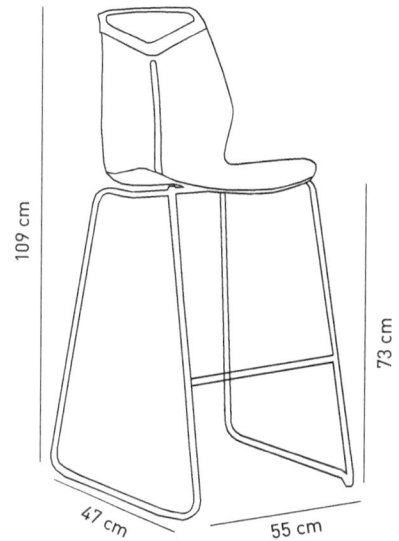

109 cm

73 cm

47 cm

55 cm

Colour Options

Cream-Orange 101020142

Cream-Dark Blue 101020148

Cream-Red 101020140

Ivory White-Red 101020898

Red-Red 101020141

Orange-Orange 101020144

Black-Black 101020269

Sax Blue-Blue 101020145

Wenge-Orange 101020143

Crtn

Net: 6,00 kg
Gross: 7,10 kg

20' DC: 240 pcs
40' DC: 480 pcs
40' HC: 560 pcs
90 cbm truck: 700 pcs

4 pcs / crtn

Scan me

Chair Stella

Chair Stella with UV ray resistant polypropylene shell. Colours: cream, ivory white, yellow, orange, red, light green, sax blue, wenge and black. Legs are anodized 20mm diameter aluminium tube to make the chair suitable for outdoor use. Chair Stella is light and stackable, suitable for use in public environments.

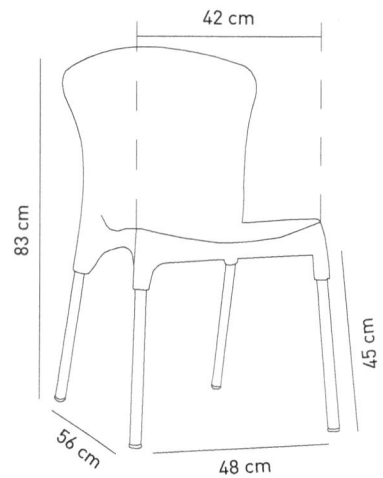

42 cm

83 cm

45 cm

56 cm

48 cm

Colour Options

☐ Ivory White 101020899
☐ Cream 101020078
☐ Yellow 101020080
☐ Orange 101020083
☐ Red 101020085
☐ Light Green 101020081
☐ Sax Blue 101020079
☐ Wenge 101020089
■ Black 101020082

	Crtn	Stack
Net:	3,05 kg	3,05 kg
Gross:	3,60 kg	3,40 kg
20' DC:	360 pcs	572 pcs
40' DC:	744 pcs	1166 pcs
40' HC:	840 pcs	1272 pcs
90 cbm truck:	1020 pcs	1560 pcs
	6 pcs / crtn	22-24 pcs / stack

Scan me

Armchair Mars

Armchair Mars is a Tilia classic, known for its perfect combination of functionality and beauty. Armchair Mars is not affected by temperature changes, is stackable up to eight elements and characterized by its enveloping comfortable seat, design elegance, practicality, cleaning ease and wide colour range such as; cream, ivory white, orange, red, light green, sax blue and black.

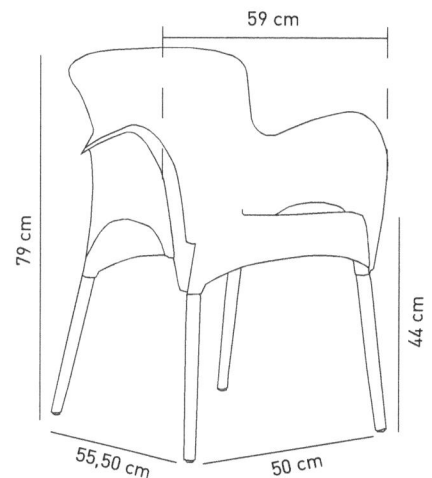

59 cm
79 cm
44 cm
55,50 cm
50 cm

Colour Options

Ivory White 101010557
Cream 101010040
Yellow 101010042
Orange 101010045
Red 101010048
Light Green 101010043
Sax Blue 101010041
Wenge 101010051
Black 101010044

	Crtn	Stack
Net:	3,55 kg	3,55 kg
Gross:	4,50 kg	3,90 kg
20' DC:	252 pcs	550 pcs
40' DC:	516 pcs	1122 pcs
40' HC:	616 pcs	1224 pcs
90 cbm truck:	728 pcs	1450 pcs
	4 pcs / crtn	22-24 pcs / stack

Scan me

Armchair Sole

Comfortable and ergonomic, Armchair Sole is made of resistant materials: polypropylene shell and anodized 20mm diameter aluminium legs. Wide colour range such as; cream, ivory white, orange, red, light green, sax blue and black. The formal solutions, materials and practicality let Armchair Sole suit indoors & outdoors and represent an excellent contract product.

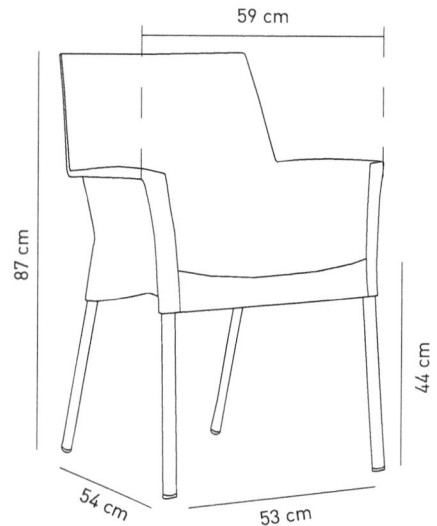

59 cm

87 cm

44 cm

54 cm

53 cm

Colour Options

☐ Ivory White 101010558
☐ Cream 101010024
☐ Yellow 101010026
◻ Orange 101010029
◻ Red 101010032
☐ Light Green 101010027
◻ Sax Blue 101010025
◼ Wenge 101010035
◼ Black 101010028

	Crtn	Stack
Net/Gross	Net: 4,00 kg Gross: 5,15 kg	Net: 4,00 kg Gross: 4,30 kg
	20' DC: 228 pcs 40' DC: 492 pcs 40' HC: 564 pcs 90 cbm truck: 664 pcs	20' DC: 408 pcs 40' DC: 816 pcs 40' HC: 912 pcs 90 cbm truck: 1188 pcs
	4 pcs / crtn	17-19 pcs / stack

Scan me

Armchair Gora

Gora, the armchair bearing the signature of Tilia's design, specially designed for the contract sector and to extend Tilia's soft line. Gora comes in cream, ivory white, yellow, orange, red, light green, sax blue and charcoal colours. Armchair Gora has a sturdy metal base, the result of the latest industrial technology. Thanks to the strong materials used, it is suitable for indoor & outdoor use.

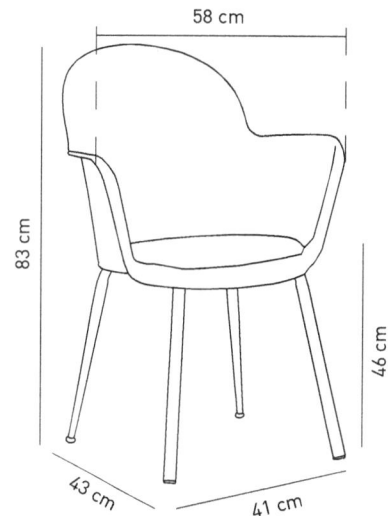

58 cm

83 cm

46 cm

43 cm

41 cm

Colour Options

- Ivory White 101010559
- Cream 101010011
- Yellow 101010013
- Orange 101010016
- Red 101010019
- Light Green 101010014
- Sax Blue 101010012
- Charcoal 101010364

Crtn

Net: 3,90 kg
Gross: 4,85 kg

20' DC: 220 pcs
40' DC: 440 pcs
40' HC: 516 pcs
90 cbm truck: 592 pcs

4 pcs / crtn

Scan me

Table Sun

Ø 70 w ekol, bouquet and antares bases

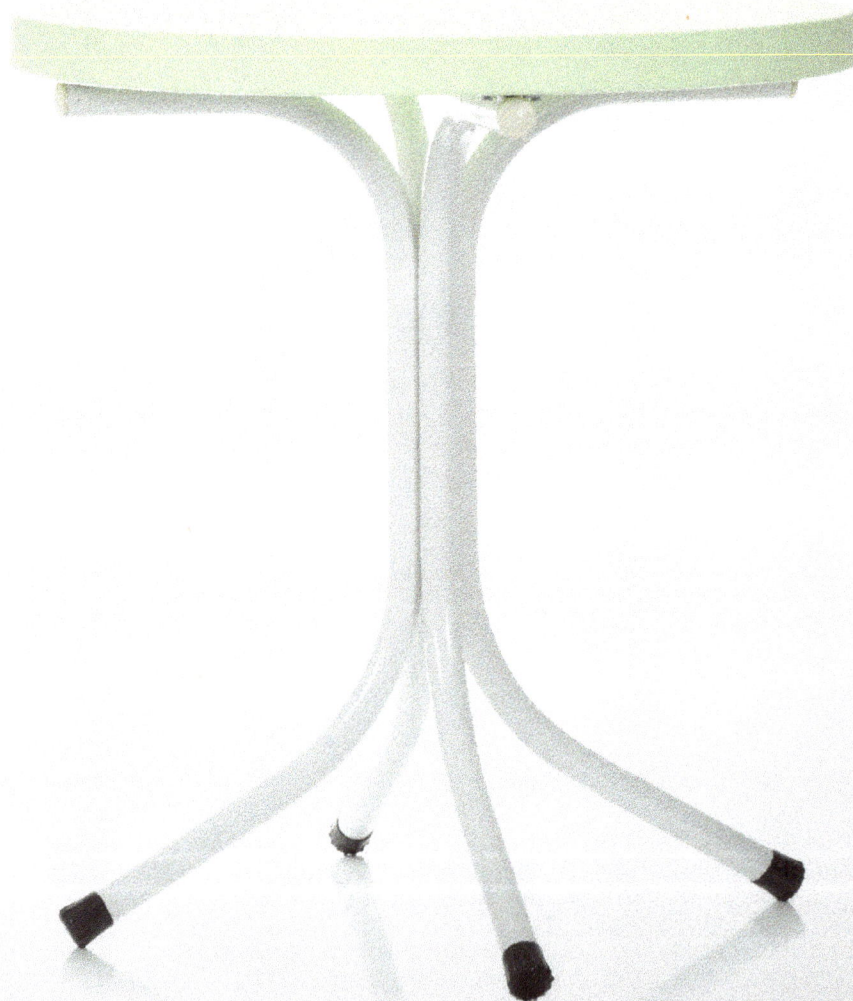

Table Sun comes in five different versions specially for outdoor use; bar base, ekol base, bouquet base, folding base and antares base. This a complete collection of tables for various uses. It comes in seven different colours; cream, white, yellow, orange, red, light green and sax blue.

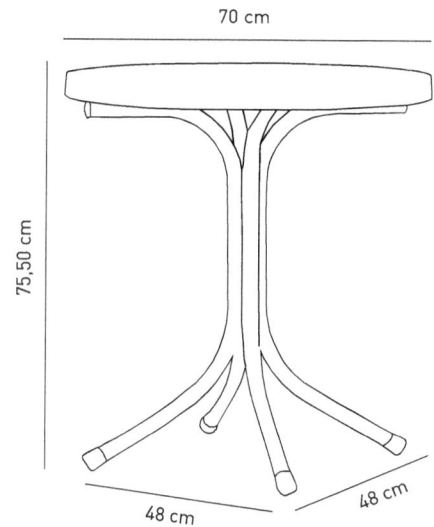

70 cm

75,50 cm

48 cm   48 cm

Colour Options

☐ Ivory White 101030216
☐ Cream 101030020
☐ Yellow 101030022
☐ Orange 101030025
☐ Red 101030026
☐ Light Green 101030023
☐ Sax Blue 101030021

Crtn

Net: 6,35 kg
Gross: 7,20 kg

20' DC: 500 pcs
40' DC: 1000 pcs
40' HC: 1100 pcs
90 cbm truck: 1200 pcs

1 pcs / crtn top
7 pcs / crtn base

Scan me

Ekol Metal Bar Base

Ekol Metal Base

Bouquet Base

Antares Base

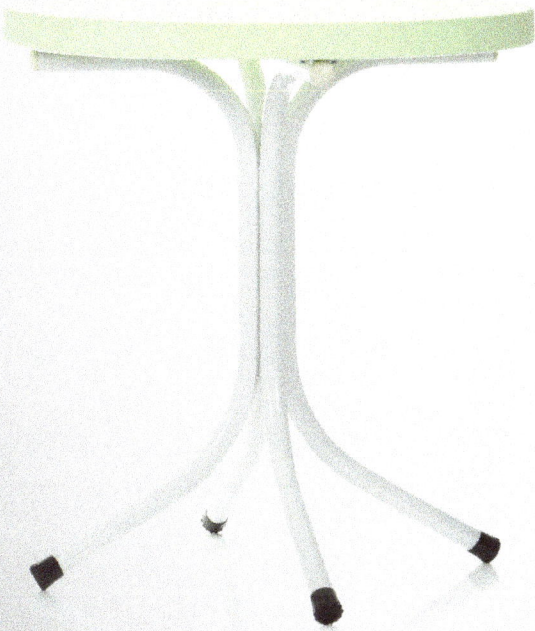

Table Capri
Square

Table Capri is surely made to please the eyes of the viewer and to complete Chair Capri with its existence. This compact table is useful in many ways, including its feet being adjustable. And the same base can be used for both round and square table tops including 69x69, 77x77, 90x90, Ø 80, Ø 90. With this convenient option, Table Capri will steal any of its user's hearts easily. Indoor usage is advised.

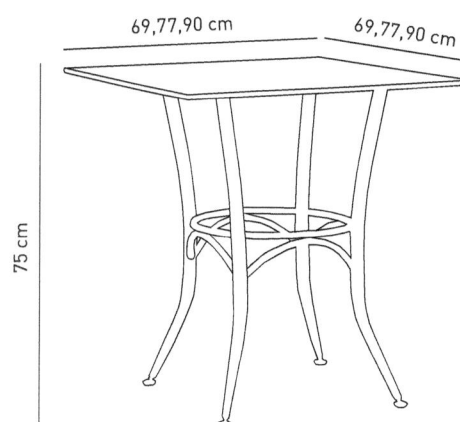

69,77,90 cm   69,77,90 cm

75 cm

Options		Crtn - 69x69	Crtn -77x77	Crtn - 90x90
White 101020659		Net: 12,60 kg	Net: 13,95 kg	Net: 18,00 kg
69x69 cm		Gross: 13,60 kg	Gross: 14,95 kg	Gross: 19,00 kg
White 101020660		20' DC: 370 pcs	20' DC: 370 pcs	20' DC: 370 pcs
77x77 cm		40' DC: 750 pcs	40' DC: 750 pcs	40' DC: 750 pcs
		40' HC: 850 pcs	40' HC: 850 pcs	40' HC: 850 pcs
		90 cbm truck: 1000 pcs	90 cbm truck: 1000 pcs	90 cbm truck: 1000 pcs
White 101020663		1 pc / crtn top	1 pc / crtn top	1 pc / crtn top
90x90 cm		7 pcs / stack base	7 pcs / stack base	7 pcs / stack base

Scan me

Table Capri
Round

Table Capri is surely made to please the eyes of the viewer and to complete Chair Capri with its existence. This compact table is useful in many ways, including its feet being adjustable. And the same base can be used for both round and square table tops including 69x69, 70x70, 90x90, Ø 80, Ø 90. With this convenient option, Table Capri will steal any of its user's hearts easily. Indoor usage is advised.

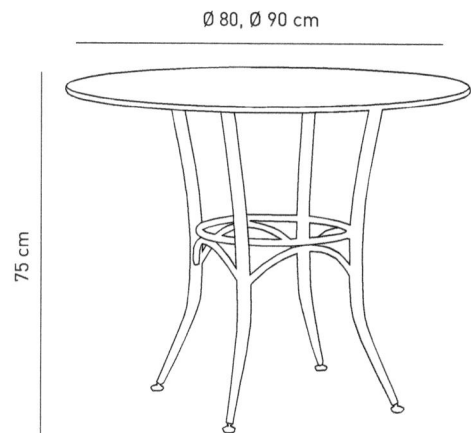

Ø 80, Ø 90 cm

75 cm

Options

☐ White 101020661
  Ø 80 cm

☐ White 101020662
  Ø 90 cm

	Crtn - Ø 80 cm	Crtn - Ø 90 cm
	Net: 12,70 kg Gross: 13,70 kg	Net: 15,10 kg Gross: 16,10 kg
	20' DC: 370 pcs 40' DC: 750 pcs 40' HC: 850 pcs 90 cbm truck: 1000 pcs	20' DC: 370 pcs 40' DC: 750 pcs 40' HC: 850 pcs 90 cbm truck: 1000 pcs
	1 pc / crtn top 7 pcs / stack base	1 pc / crtn top 7 pcs / stack base

Scan me

Table Capri

Rectangle

Table Capri with the rectangle table top not only pleases the eyes of the viewer but also convenient for those who like to gather a lot of people around the same table. This compact table is useful in many ways, including its feet being adjustable. With its completing factor with Chair Capri, Table Capri will steal any of its user's hearts easily. Indoor usage is advised.

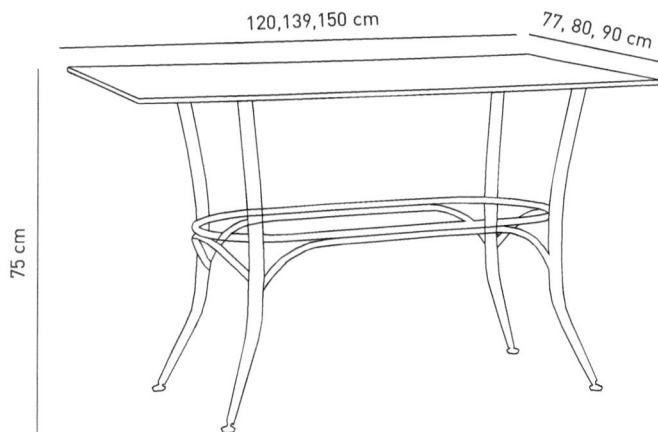

120,139,150 cm

77, 80, 90 cm

75 cm

Options	Crtn - 77x120	Crtn -80x139	Crtn - 90x150
☐ White 101020664	Net: 20,60 kg	Net: 24,00 kg	Net: 27,90 kg
77x120 cm	Gross: 21,60 kg	Gross: 25,00 kg	Gross: 28,90 kg
☐ White 101020665	20' DC: 260 pcs	20' DC: 260 pcs	20' DC: 260 pcs
80x139 cm	40' DC: 520 pcs	40' DC: 520 pcs	40' DC: 520 pcs
	40' HC: 630 pcs	40' HC: 630 pcs	40' HC: 630 pcs
	90 cbm truck: 750 pcs	90 cbm truck: 750 pcs	90 cbm truck: 750 pcs
☐ White 101020666	1 pcs / crtn top	1 pcs / stack	1 pcs / stack
90x150 cm	2 pcs / stack base	2 pcs / stack base	2 pcs / stack base

Scan me

Sunbed Maris

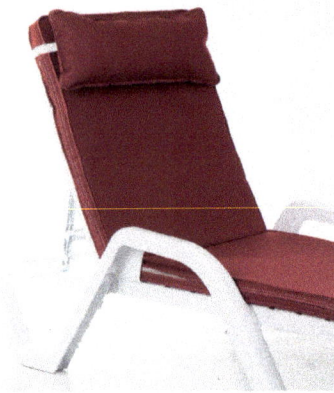

Sunlounger Maris with arm and comes in two different colors; wood and white. Tubular frame produced from polypropylene, stackable up to 25 pieces, back reclining in 5 different positions.

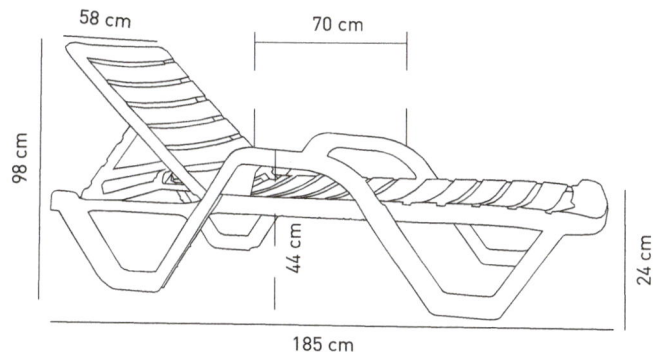

58 cm
70 cm
98 cm
44 cm
24 cm
185 cm

Colour Options

☐ Ivory White 101040015

◼ Wood 101040003

Waterproof Fabric Options (Outdoor)

☐ White

☐ Beige

◼ Red

◼ Orange

◼ Claret

◼ Yellow

◼ Blue

◼ Green

Sunbed Maris

Net: 9,80 kg
Gross: 10,00 kg

20' DC: 225 pcs
40' DC: 475 pcs
40' HC: 546 pcs
90 cbm truck: 600 pcs

25-28 pcs / stack

Cushion Maris

Net: 2,00 kg
Gross: 2,10 kg

20' DC: 450 pcs
40' DC: 900 pcs
40' HC: 1100 pcs
90 cbm truck: 1250 pcs

5 pcs / package

Scan me

Sunbed Mare
With Armrest

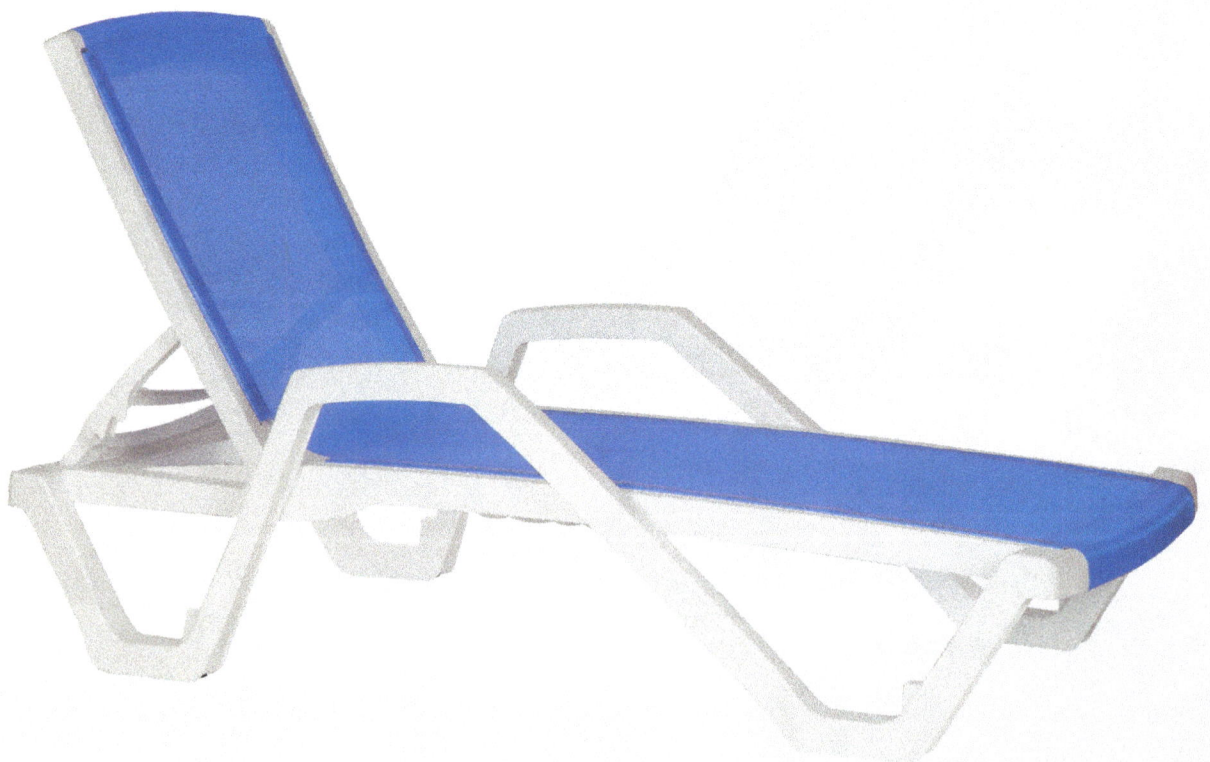

It is a charming model from Tilia. Sunbed Mare consists of 100% virgin polypropylene mixed with breathable and flexible synthetic fabric (net). It comes in with various matching colours such as; ivory white/beige, white/blue, wenge/beige, ivory white/yellow and green/beige. Stackable up to 20 pieces, back reclining in 4 different positions.

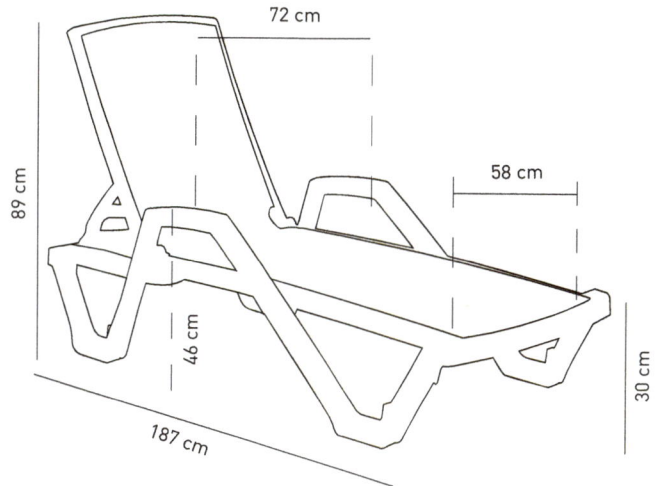

Colour Options

Ivory White & Beige 106010254
Ivory White & Blue 106010255
Ivory White & Yellow 106010256
Wood & Beige 106010031
Green & Beige 106010026

Net Colours

Beige
Yellow
Blue

Stack

Net: 10,50 kg
Gross: 10,70 kg

20' DC: 162 pcs
40' DC: 324 pcs
40' HC: 360 pcs
90 cbm truck: 400 pcs

18-20 pcs / stack

Scan me

Sunbed Mare

Without Armrest

It is a charming model from Tilia. Sunbed Mare consists of 100% virgin polypropylene mixed with breathable and flexible synthetic fabric (net). It comes in with various matching colours such as; ivory white/beige, ivory white/blue, wenge/beige, ivory white/yellow and green/beige. Stackable up to 20 pieces, back reclining in 4 different positions.

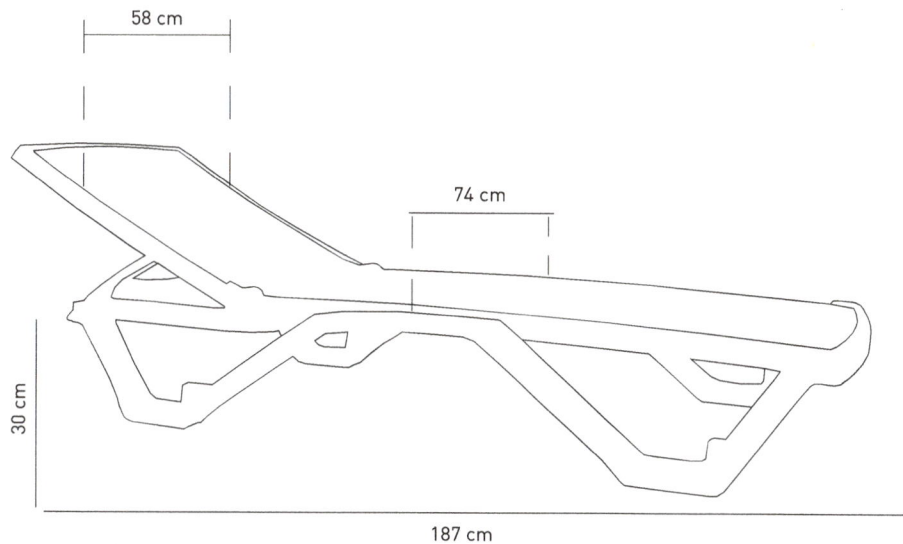

58 cm

74 cm

30 cm

187 cm

Colour Options

Ivory White & Beige 106010257
Ivory White & Blue 106010258
Ivory White & Yellow 106010259
Wood & Beige 106010029
Green & Beige 106010030

Net Colours

Beige
Yellow
Blue

Stack

Net: 10,30 kg
Gross: 10,50 kg

20' DC: 180 pcs
40' DC: 360 pcs
40' HC: 418 pcs
90 cbm truck: 460 pcs

20-22 pcs / stack

Scan me

Table Base Antares
Single & Double

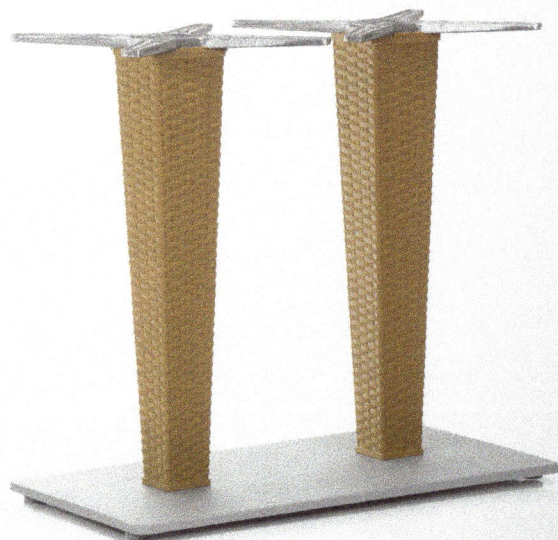

The tube is made from 100% virgin polypropylene and the base is made of aluminium. It is adjustable with non-slip pingos. You can combine with Table Antares 70x70, 80x80, 80x120 and 90x150. It comes with six different colours ; black, wood, wenge, cream, coffee and ivory white.

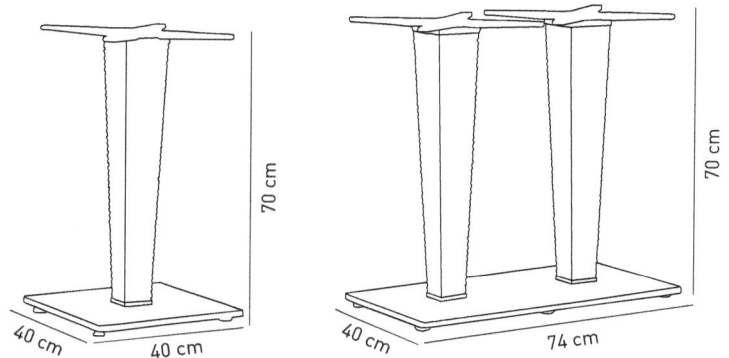

70 cm 40 cm 40 cm

70 cm 40 cm 74 cm

Colour Options-**Single**	Colour Options-**Double**		Crtn-**Single**	Crtn-**Double**
☐ Ivory White 202020059	☐ Ivory White 202010044	Net: 8,20 kg	Net: 18,00 kg
☐ Cream 202020081	☐ Cream 202010046	Gross: 9,00 kg	Gross: 19,00 kg
◻ Wood 202020082	◻ Wood 202010045	20' DC: 750 pcs	20' DC: 350 pcs
◻ Coffee 202010041	◻ Coffee 202010048	40' DC: 1500 pcs	40' DC: 700 pcs
◼ Wenge 202020058	◼ Wenge 202010038	40' HC: 1750 pcs	40' HC: 830 pcs
◼ Black 202020088	◼ Black 202010047	90 cbm truck: 2000 pcs	90 cbm truck: 950 pcs
		2 crtns / set	2 crtns / set

Coffee Table Erba

Small side table in perfect 49x49x44 cm size. Colourful, practical, safe and functional. You can combine it with Sunbed Mare & Sunbed Maris. Stackable up to 15 pieces, and has removable legs. It comes in six different colours; ivory white, cream, wood, coffee, wenge and black.

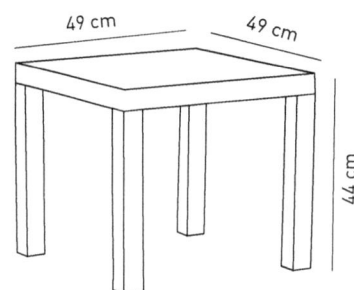

Colour Options

☐ Ivory White 101030217
☐ Cream 101030035
■ Wood 101030032
■ Coffee 101030211
■ Wenge 101030172
■ Black 101030210

Crtn

Net: 1,90 kg
Gross: 2,10 kg

20' DC: 1850 pcs
40' DC: 3700 pcs
40' HC: 4300 pcs
90 cbm truck: 4900 pcs

5 pcs / crtn

Coffee Table Monoblock

Side table. It is totally one piece product, easy to carry and stack. It comes in six different colours; cream, ivory white, wood, coffee, wenge and black.

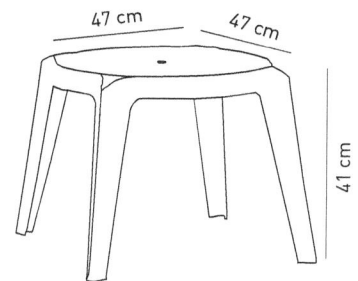

47 cm   47 cm

41 cm

Colour Options

☐ Ivory White 106010260
☐ Cream 106010020
▨ Wood 106010180
▨ Coffee 106010261
■ Wenge 106010019
■ Black 106010021

Stack

Net: 1,45 kg
Gross: 1,55 kg

20' DC: 1400 pcs
40' DC: 2800 pcs
40' HC: 3300 pcs
90 cbm truck: 3800 pcs

32 pcs / stack

Coffee Table Antares

It is the lightest product in Antares family. It has rattan looking design with six different colours; Black, wood, wenge, cream, coffee and ivory white. It is stackable up to 40 pcs. Useful for both indoor & outdoor.

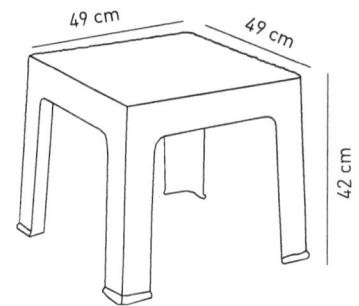

49 cm 49 cm 42 cm

Colour Options

☐ Ivory White 101030218
☐ Cream 101030128
☐ Wood 101030127
☐ Coffee 101030219
☐ Wenge 101030120
☐ Black 101030129

Stack

Net: 1,40 kg
Gross: 1,50 kg

20' DC: 1800 pcs
40' DC: 3600 pcs
40' HC: 4300 pcs
90 cbm truck: 4800 pcs

40 pcs / stack

This magazine may be ordered through booksellers or by contacting

iBooExport
"Reach the World "

Istanbul Office	London Office
EGS Business Park	3rd Floor
B2 Blok No: 12 D.01	86-90 Paul Street
Yesilkoy, Bakirkoy,	London
İstanbul 34149	EC2A 4NE
Turkey	United Kingdom
t: +90 850 460 1 064	t: +44 20 3828 7097

info@ibooexport.com II www.ibooexport.com

ISBN

978-1-947144-80-4 (sc)
978-1-947144-81-1 (e)

We care about the environment. This paper used in this publication is both acid-free and totally chlorine-free (TCF). It meets the minimum requirements of ANSI/NISO z39.48-1992 (r 1997)

Printed in the USA

www.ingramcontent.com/pod-product-compliance
Lightning Source LLC
Chambersburg PA
CBHW052347210326
41597CB00037B/6286